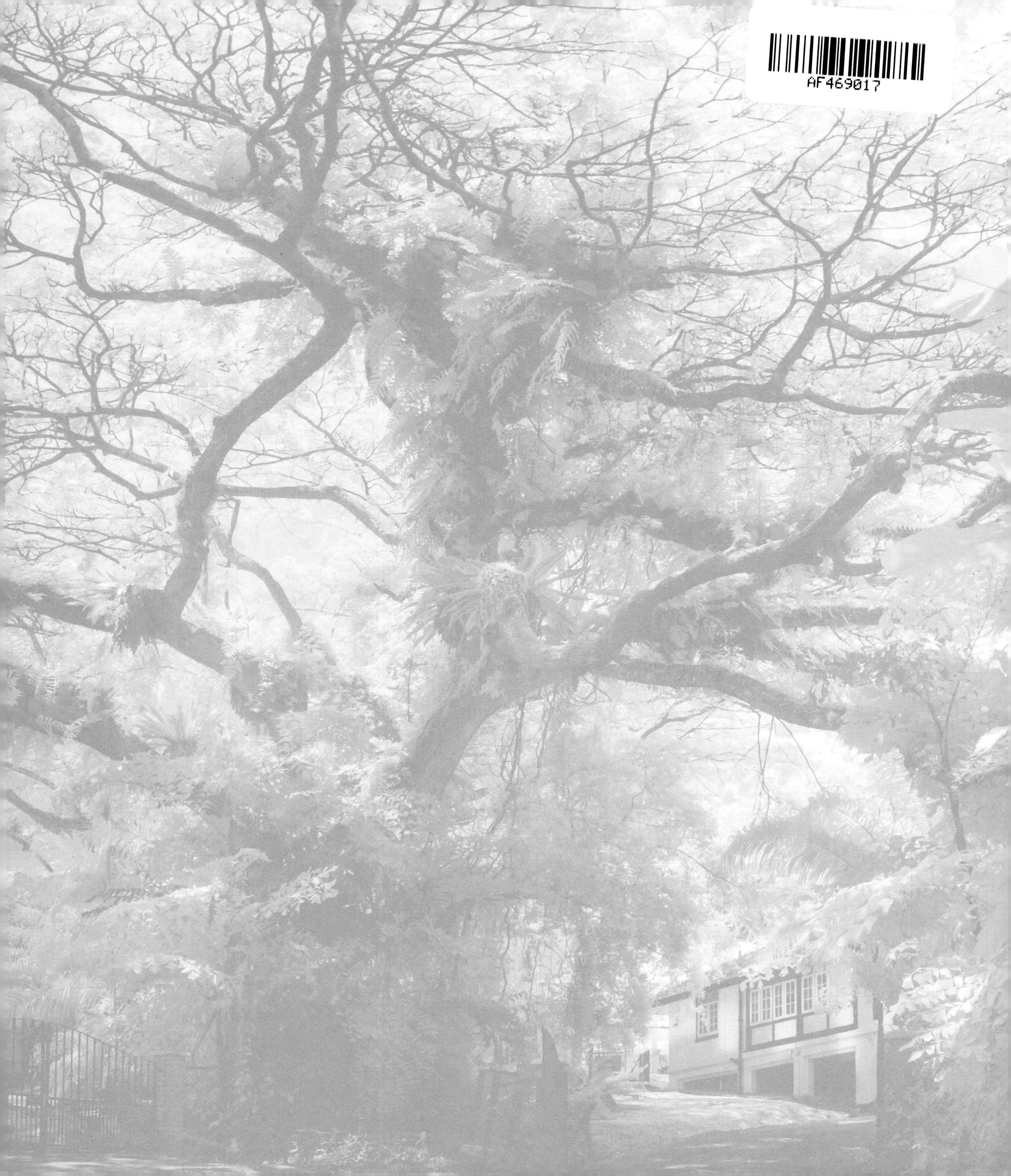

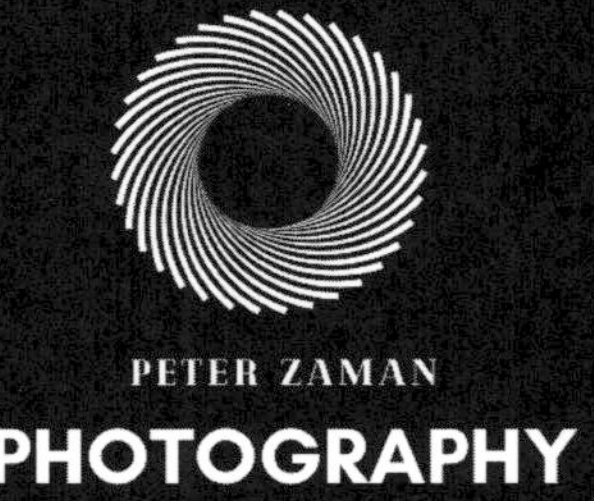
PETER ZAMAN
PHOTOGRAPHY

The Black & White Project

Unseen Landscapes of Singapore

Photographs by

Peter Zaman

Foreword by

Dr Julian Davison

Index of Photographs

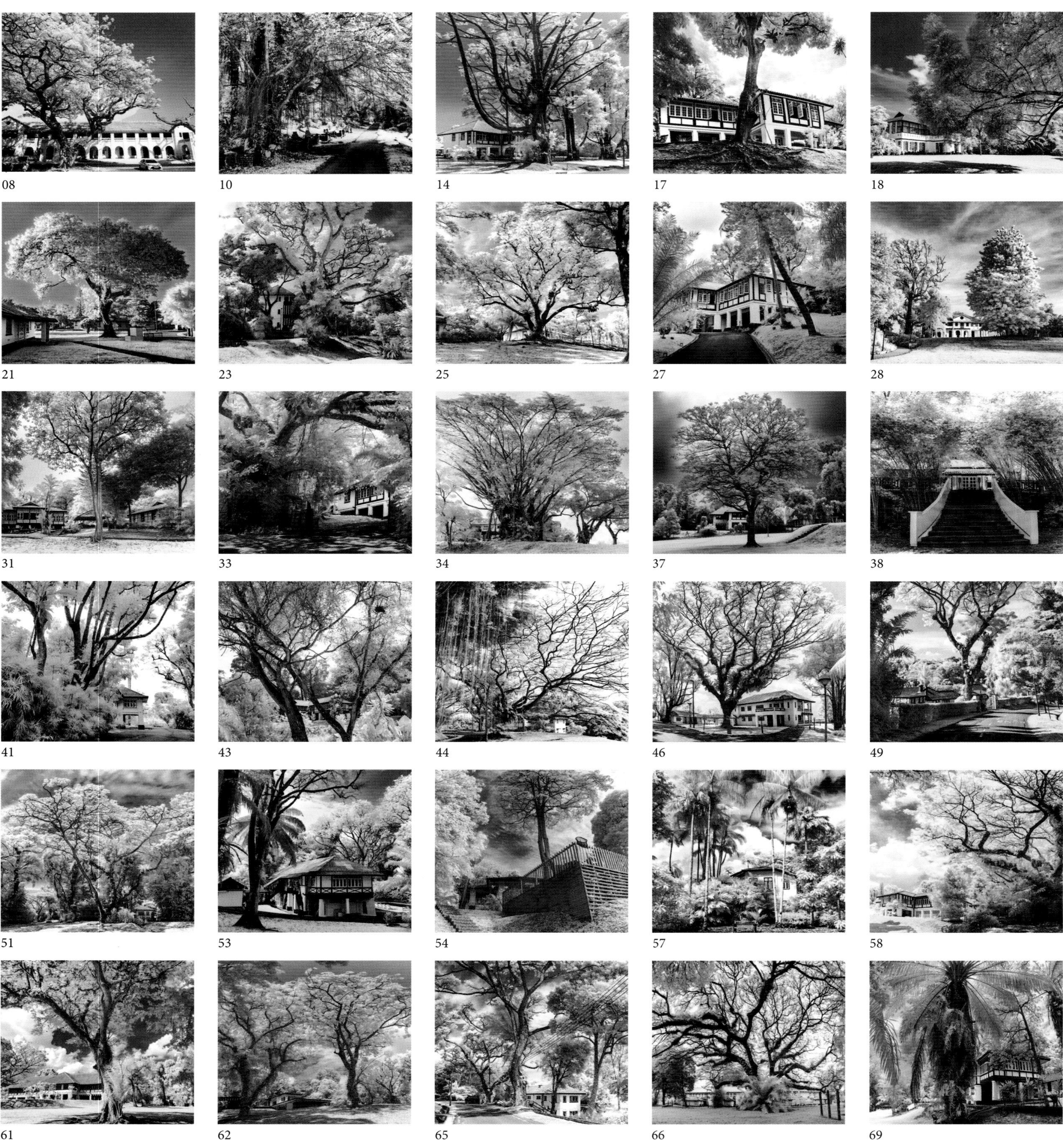

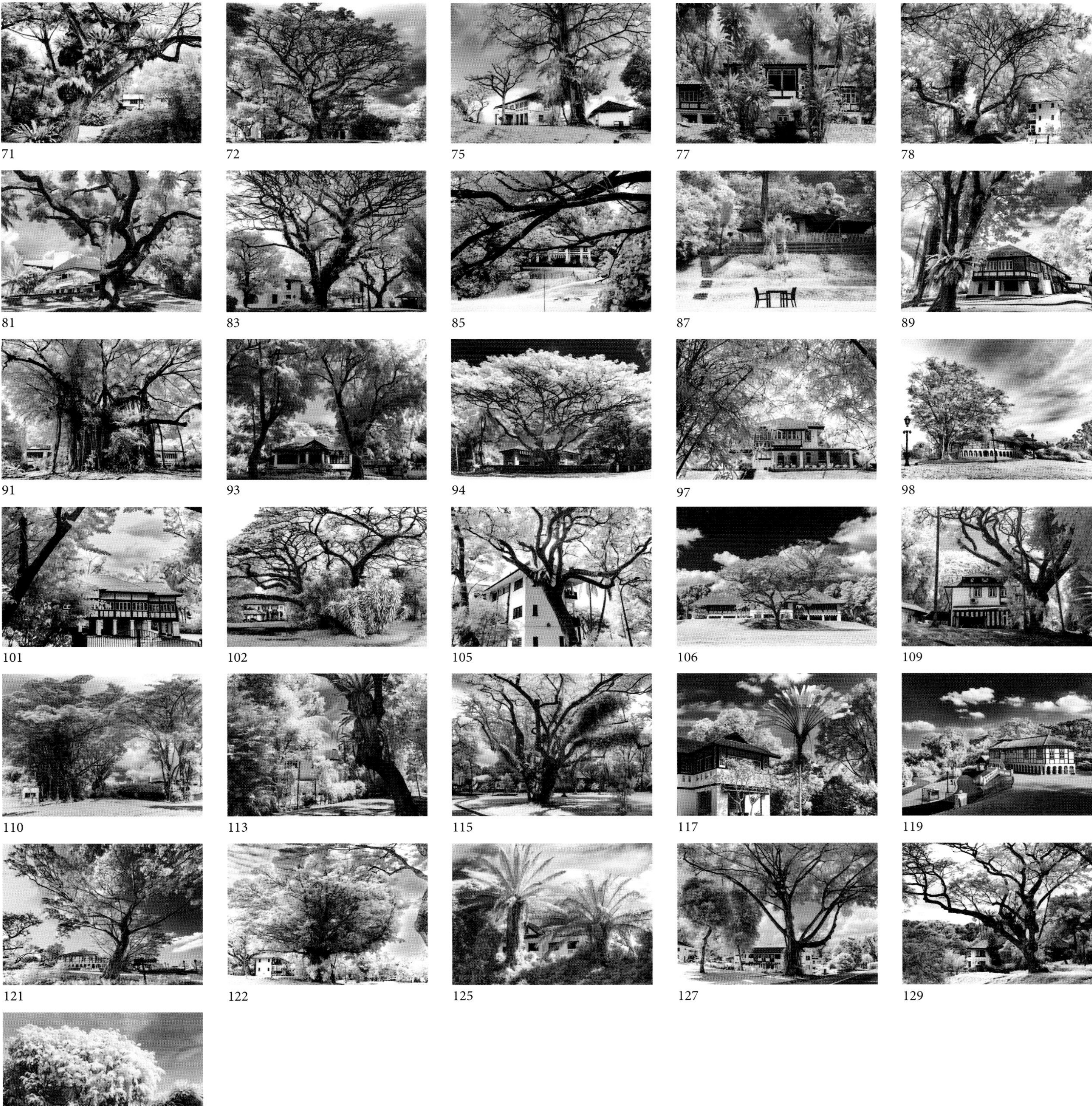

71 72 75 77 78
81 83 85 87 89
91 93 94 97 98
101 102 105 106 109
110 113 115 117 119
121 122 125 127 129
130

Foreword

THE BLACK AND WHITE Singapore house has come to be seen as the quintessential home of the expatriate Englishman during the British era and in this respect it occupies a special place in both the architectural and social history of Singapore. Like the Anglo-Indian bungalow to which it is related, the black and white house is a hybrid form of architecture, a building where East does indeed meet West, "tho' they come from the ends of the earth". On the one hand, there are the overtly European references — the Doric columns and Classical detailing — which leave little doubt that these were once the homes of Singapore's colonial elite. But then again, these were houses that were intended for tropical living and they were designed to fit that purpose. In its essentials, then, the archetypal black and white house is perhaps best thought of as a late-Victorian or Edwardian home, reimagined in an Eastern setting.

The most obvious oriental influences are of course those of British India: the broad verandahs, widespread eaves and tall, double-leafed, shuttered door and window openings, are all characteristic features of the Anglo-Indian bungalow. Malay references are also in evidence. These are most clearly seen in the case of single-storey dwellings, which are raised up off the ground on brick piers. This was a trick that was almost certainly borrowed from Malay architecture, the idea here being to make the most of ambient breezes as a means of natural ventilation, while keeping one's feet dry in the rainy season. Together these make up the Asian component of these houses.

When it comes to matters of architectural style, however, the more important elements derive from what was considered fashionable in Britain in the latter part of the nineteenth century. As one might expect, there is a strong Arts and Crafts vibe, combined with a late Victorian enthusiasm for half-timbered, Tudor-style country houses. The two went hand-in-hand, since they both drew their inspiration from traditional English vernacular architectural styles and artisanal construction techniques. — what was a lovingly referred to as 'Olde English'. Admittedly, one would be hard-pressed to find much evidence of mock-Tudor features in the surviving architectural record of Singapore, the odd half-timbered gable aside. It was, nonetheless, a defining feature of the earliest black and white houses, when they started to appear around the turn of the last century. Sadly, most of these buildings were pulled down long ago in the endless cycle of demolition and renewal which underpins the narrative of Singapore's architectural history. The idea lingers on, however, like a ghostly presence, and it is, of course, precisely this same ghostly presence, which endows the black and white house with a quintessential 'Englishness' that is such an integral part of their appeal; the black and white house is very much a 'Home Thoughts from Abroad' style or architecture.

That nostalgia, or a longing for a distant homeland, should have a part to play in all of this is readily understandable when one considers that these houses belong to a period when the typical tour of duty for an expat Englishman in the Far East was anything between three to five years. This was a long time to be absent from one's native land and naturally any kind of device that might assuage the occasional pang of homesickness was eagerly seized upon: the black and white house was one way of making oneself literally feel 'at home' in a foreign land.

* * *

A large part of the charm of the black and white house lies in their setting, viz. an attractively 'wooded' landscape, with a long driveway cut between mossy banks and ferns; a house placed on rising ground

“God Almighty first planted a garden. And indeed, it is the purest of human pleasures.”

Francis Bacon (1561–1626)

or at the summit of a modest eminence; a swathe of green lawn with a dark wall of trees behind; dense thickets of jungle undergrowth; a tall stand of Nibong Palms, their feathery fronds silhouetted against the sky; brightly-coloured beds of canna lilies and the ubiquitous Heliconia in all its many forms — Firecracker, Parrots Peak and Lobster Claw. Captain John Dill Northwood, writing in 1898, had good reason to reflect that “whatever may be thought of the town of Singapore, it must be admitted that the suburbs and surrounding country are charming. Tanglin is hard to beat and a Singapore house, embowered in fernery, amidst pretty lawns and beautiful trees, forms a very attractive and pleasing picture.”

This “attractive and pleasing picture” did not occur by accident. Despite the apparent “naturalness” of the verdant tropical setting in which we are accustomed to finding the black and white house situated, there was nothing incidental about these landscapes. Rather, a lot of thought was given as to how their grounds should be laid out and planted. And here it was the English landscape garden, otherwise known as “English parkland”, which was the starting point.

* * *

The English landscape garden was a phenomenon of the eighteenth and early nineteenth centuries. The guiding ethos was one that sought an engagement with the natural world, rather a command performance, which was the thinking behind the Tudor and Renaissance gardens that preceded them. In Elizabethan times, the natural world was viewed as something to be conquered, to be reined in, mastered and made to do man’s bidding, a realm that was subordinate to the “Empire of Man” — the phrase comes from Francis Bacon (1561–1626), the leading philosopher of that age, who believed that man must dominate nature if he wished to survive. This ‘expropriatory’ approach to nature was reflected in gardens that were laid out as geometrical spaces, with criss-crossing walkways and rectangular parterres (levelled areas with flowerbeds). Also an abundance of topiary: bushes and shrubbery cut into regular geometric forms — box hedges, spheres, cones, even pyramids — or else shaped like animals.

This was nature tamed; the wilderness domesticated and placed at mankind’s service. The eighteenth century landscape garden was completely contrary to this. Here, the prevailing aesthetic was an appreciation of the naturalness of nature — there was a special term for this: *Natura naturata* — where delight was taken in the organic randomness of nature, in all its wild fecundity.

The foremost exponent of the English landscape garden is of course Lancelot “Capability” Brown (1718–1783), often lauded as “England’s greatest gardener”. He was nicknamed “Capability” because he was fond of telling his landed clients that their estates had great “capability” for improvement, And improve them he did, by exploiting the existing topography of a site, to which he either added or subtracted as he saw fit: Brown’s landscaping often entailed massive earthworks, the damming of streams, the rerouting of roads and thoroughfares, even the demolition of entire villages if they interfered with his grand vision of a perfectly realised landscape. The end result was broad swathes of lawn merging seamlessly with the surrounding countryside, reflecting lakes that filled the bottom of a steep valley, wooded hillsides reaching to the skyline — this was what Capability Brown was good at arranging.

This being the eighteenth century, many of Brown’s clients were men of substance, wealthy aristocrats who had enjoyed the benefits of a Classical education — in their youth, had been on a Grand Tour of the Continent, they had visited Rome and Florence, they had read their Horace and Virgil, in Latin of course. Accordingly, we find Brown's landscapes punctuated with carefully placed Roman temples, Palladian bridges and other Classical ornaments. This was very much in keeping with the spirit of the age, but it was Nature unadorned that Brown loved best: the play of light on water and trees, the contours of the land, a sweeping vista and a distant horizon — these were the tools that he preferred to work with.

* * *

Brown's vision was the eighteenth-century acme of pastoral pleasure, refracted through the lens of Classical allusion and early Romantic tendencies, and it cast a long, though not unpleasing, shadow across the English landscape for a century and a half. The ultimate expression of this aesthetic in Singapore is of course the Botanic Gardens, which were first laid out in 1859, though they have since been enlarged many times over, the most recent addition being the Gallop Extension of 2021. Although they have long had an economic garden attached to them for the propagation and dissemination of "useful" plants, not least the rubber tree, the Singapore Botanic Gardens initially started out as a "pleasure garden" and ornamental park to be enjoyed by the members of the Singapore Agri-horticultural Society who were responsible for their instigation.

They were laid out by their first Superintendent, a Scottish gentleman by the name of Lawrence Niven who was the manager of a neighbouring nutmeg plantation. Born into a family of gardeners, Niven appears to have served an apprenticeship at Rossdhu House, on the shores of Loch Lomond, whose gardens were designed by Thomas White, a renowned eighteenth-century landscape gardener who had himself trained under Capability Brown. Certainly it is possible to discern a very strong Brownian influence in the design of Singapore's Botanic Gardens, which have remained remarkably unchanged since they were first laid down by Niven back in the 1860s. William Sproston Caine, Member of Parliament for Barrow-on-Furness and a keen horticulturalist, visited the Botanic Gardens in 1887 and found them to be "... beautifully situated on the sunny slope of an evergreen hill, the most delightful garden imaginable, nearer to Eden than I could have believed anything on earth to be" *(A Trip Around the World in 1887-8).*

To what extent the Botanic Gardens may have influenced the design of other Singapore gardens is difficult to gauge. The landscaping of the grounds surrounding Government House, today's Istana, which were laid out at around the same time as the Botanic Gardens, clearly conform to the same aesthetic. Ultimately, it was all part of the mid-nineteenth century horticultural zeitgeist, which subsequently became the default garden style of Singapore up until the outbreak of the war in the Pacific: the military encampments that were built in the 1930s as war with Japan grew increasingly likely — Alexandra Park and Sembawang, for example — are laid out in a manner that would surely have meet with Lawrence Niven's approval.

Ideological musings aside, there is also Singapore's gently undulating topography to consider, which was practically an English landscape gardener's dreamscape come true. Though many have since been razed to provide infill for modern Singapore's ever expanding coastline, in the nineteenth century there were hills simply everywhere, each one the perfect situation for a breezy belvedere with fine views over the surrounding countryside. John Cameron, one time editor of the *Straits Times*, writing in 1865, explained that while houses nearer the centre of town, where land was more pricey, "are built tolerably close together, with perhaps one or two acres each; those at a greater distance are more apart, generally crowning the summits of the innumerable little hills, which are such a geological peculiarity of Singapore, either covered with patches of jungle, or planted with nutmeg and fruit trees." He continues: "these little round hills or *bukits*, as they are termed by the Malays, give a very singular and very pleasing appearance to the island." The German naturalist and ethnologist, Dr Andreas Jagor, who visited Singapore several times between 1857 and 1861, also mentions these hill-top retreats: "almost all the great merchants have a house outside the town," he writes, "usually on the top of a hill, where the sea breeze blows through all the rooms and cools them." These country houses, he adds, "were the most pleasant and suited to their purpose that I have known in hot countries,"

Which brings us to the substance of this book, namely the special relationship that exists between the black and white Singapore house and its surroundings. This is an aspect of the black and white house that has often been overlooked in the past, but which is admirably addressed by Peter Zaman's splendid photographs of black and white houses in their garden settings. Though there is a black and white house in every image, they seldom hog the limelight. Rather, they are featured as almost as a 'natural' adjunct of the landscape, like one of William Kent's artfully placed temples, or a Palladian bridge by Capability Brown.

More often than not, it is a tree which takes pride of place in these images, a lofty Tembusu *(Crytophyllum fragrans)*, with is spreading lateral branches, being very much the local counterpart of the Lebanese Cedar, for which Capability Brown had a great fondness — his 'signature' tree, one might say. Rain Trees *(Samanea saman)* also feature strongly. Though an imported species — they are native to Central and Southern America — the Rain Tree derives its common name from a literal transcription of the Malay words *pokok hujan*. The latter refers to a remarkable feature of their leaves, which fold up on themselves on rainy days, the better to let the rainfall reach their roots, which radiate out from the base of the tree like dendrons. (The tree is alternatively referred to locally as the *pokok pukul lima*, or 'five o'clock tree', since its leaves also fold at around five in the evening, so as to make the most of the nightly precipitation of dew.) And then of course there is also is the magnificent Banyan Tree *(Ficus spp.)*, with its cat's cradle of adventitious 'prop' roots and mythical associations that connect it to the sacred tree beneath whose branches the Gautama Buddha achieved his enlightenment. (As it happens, most Fig Trees in Singapore are either natives species or else the Burmese Banyan, *Ficus kurzil*, Moraceae, rather than the Indian bodhi tree of Buddhist legend, but this need not detract from their mythical subtext.)

Tembusu, Rain Tree and Fig — there are many other trees that could be mentioned here, but these are the three arboreal species that dominate the pages of this book and which, like the black and white house in whose gardens they grow, consitute such an indelible part of the Singaporean landscape. In presenting us with these beautiful photographs, Mr Zaman has done us a great service by revealing the black and white house in a new light. Or perhaps one should say a forgotten light, for surely this was how these houses were originally intended to be seen and experienced, brimming with nostalgic references to a distant homeland at several thousand miles removed. The garden, with its Romantic English parkland resonances, was very much a part of the ensemble, while the natural topography of the island also lent a helping hand — a kind of native genius or "spirit of place" that elided home and abroad, beneath a tropic sun. In this last respect, Singapore was certainly "very capable" as Mr Brown would have it.

Dr Julian Davison

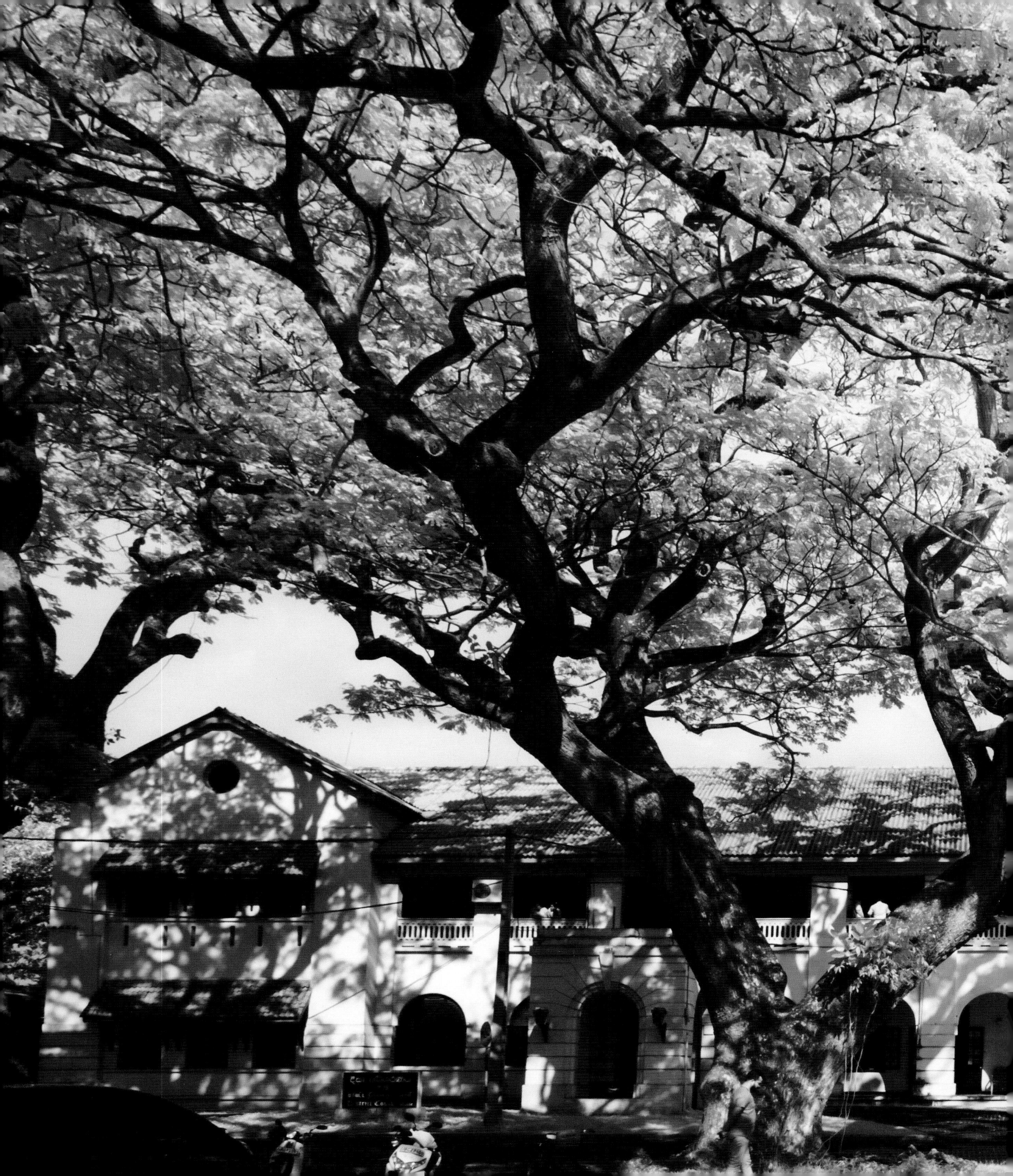

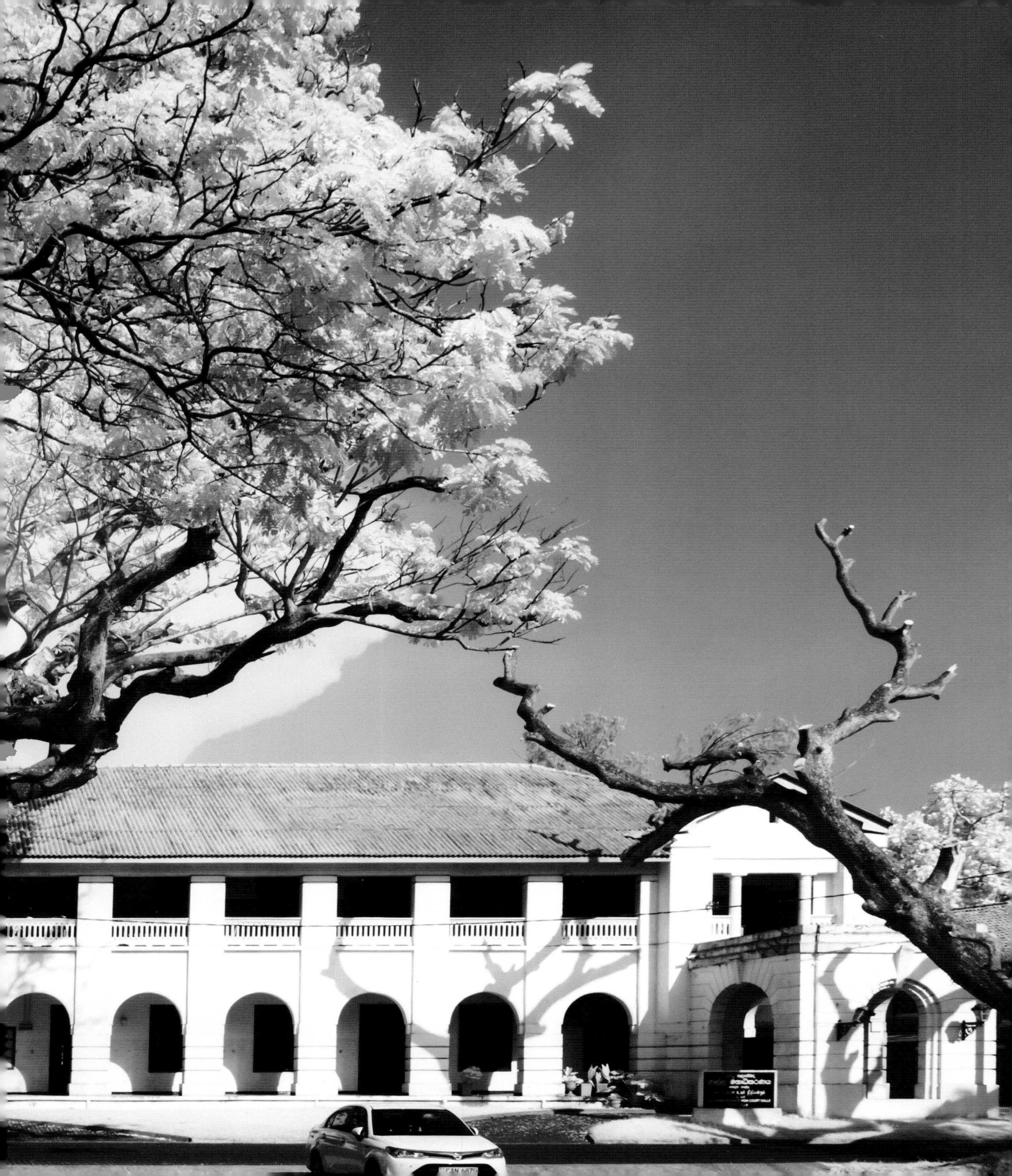

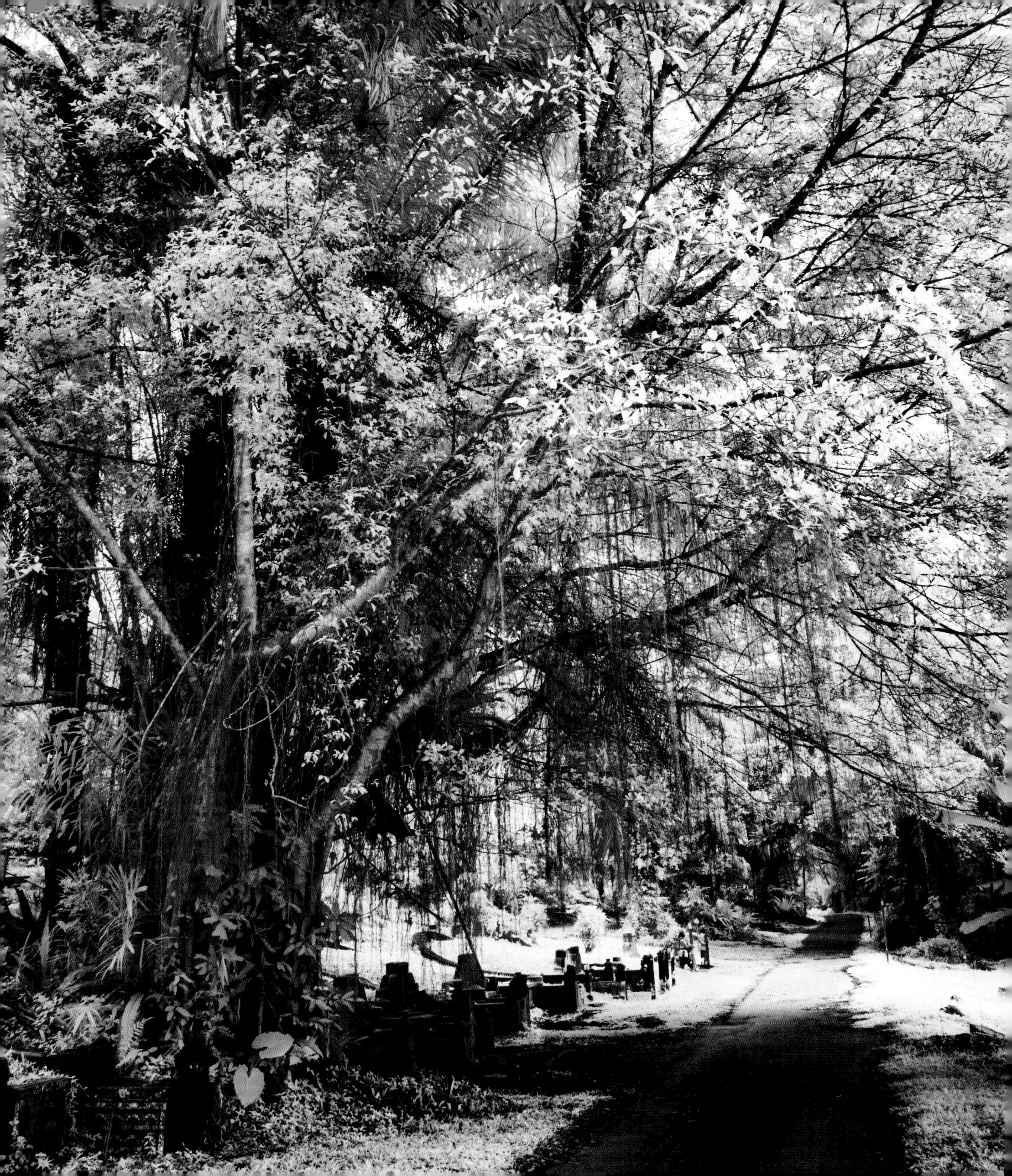

Preface

My journey as a photographer began at the age of 16 when I took my father's Yashica SLR camera and, without asking him, decided it was to be mine. Little did I realise that my photographic journey of exploration that started then, would still be continuing more than 35 years later.

Along the way, I have shifted to digital photography and experimented with different disciplines of photography. I've discovered the disciplines that I like and which, in turn, seem to like me back. Don't get me wrong, a decent photographer can adapt to and master more than one discipline and take a half decent photo; but usually the audience works out pretty quickly in which discipline they excel.

I have a natural curiosity about different techniques and approaches to photography and like to learn from other photographers whose work I respect and admire. My heroes of photography are the sources of my inspiration. Legends such as Ansel Adams, Andre Kertesz and Henri Cartier Bresson amazed me with their command of light and shadows. Modern day heroes like John McDemott, Martin Reeves and Colby Brown allowed me to see the landscape in front of me with a completely different eye. Sometimes, you just get bowled over by an image that another photographer has taken. At first you scratch your head in admiration but that then inspires a challenge to emulate and, if possible, top. It is through this process of self-challenge, that I continue to grow at what I do. As a photographer, my joy comes from contemplating an image and then finding a way to convert that into the printed reality.

Singapore has been my home since 2016 when I moved here from London. This 'garden city' certainly lives up to its name as, despite its modern edifice, it retains a deep respect for nature and green spaces. You see this when you first land at Changi airport and are brought into town via the line of majestic Rain Tree that adorn both sides of the East Coast Parkway. You soon learn about Singapore's history as a plantation for rubber, spices and other crops and why its Botanic Garden is today a UNESCO World Heritage site. As you start to look, you begin to discover ancient and majestic trees everywhere.

One of my most pleasant Singapore memories was, for the first time, coming across Alexandra Park. I was immediately smitten. On reflection, I think this was partially caused by my nostalgia for the UK and seeing Surrey-like landscapes with so many majestic local trees right in the heart of Singapore. To see such landscapes, married together with the unique Singapore construct that is the black and white house, was simply magical.

The black and white house seemed to me to be an amalgamation of an English mock-Tudor house, with an Indian bungalow but raised above the ground to fit with the old Malay architectural style. It was definitely English but also uniquely Singaporean in character. I then sought out other similar black and white estates such as Ridley Park, Mount Pleasant, Adam Park, Seletar and Malcolm Park to name but a few.

My first instinct was to try to shoot the houses in colour, as the contrast between the lush green surroundings and the white walls of the black and whites offered potentially lovely compositions. However, photographing in colour, in a country so close to the equator, means that the golden hour light sought after by landscape photographers like myself, is fleeting. The restriction in accessing these conservation houses, managed by the Singapore Land Authority and rented out to the public, made it obvious that photographing them, at their best, would be an extreme endeavour. Besides, Julian Davison's book, Black and White: *The Singapore House 1898 — 1941* with photographs by Luca Invernizzi Tettoni, had already captured some great images of the black and white houses of Singapore.

So my solution to solve the golden hour light problem was to photograph in black and white instead of colour. The photographer Ted Grant once said, "when you photograph people in colour, you photograph their clothes. But when you photograph people in black and white, you photograph their souls." I think a similar truth applies to photographing nature in black and white. When you photograph objects in nature, devoid of colour, you are photographing their essence.

When the pandemic struck in early 2020 and border-closures restricted our travel outside Singapore for almost two years, I was gifted an opportunity that became this Black and White Project. I set myself a challenge, to find a way to photograph the majestic Singapore trees together with the black and white houses, in a landscape composition.

My final solution, as you see in the pages of this book, came through a combination of trial and error and the merger of lessons learnt from other photography disciplines and techniques. The reaction I most often got when I first showed my prints from this project to anyone, was a disbelief that these images were of places in Singapore. That reaction inspired the strapline for this book.

There are probably two defining images that resulted in the final approach I took towards the photos in this book.

The first was an image I took at the Bukit Brown Cemetery showing an ancient tree with a row of graves next to a path. It was an eerie, almost ethereal, image. I was very pleased with the effect and the image. However, when I printed it to show my wife, she observed that it made for a rather morbid reminder and so might not be everyone's cup of tea.

The second was a photo I took a few years ago in Galle, Sri Lanka of a colonial-era administrative building with a large tree in front of it. As a reference to colonial era architecture, I really liked that image and wondered if I could combine those two images into a single composition using black and white houses. The Bukit Brown and Galle images are the two images immediately preceding this preface.

I tried a number of different compositions. Eventually, a single image persuaded me that I had finally found a compositional approach that works. That image started my hunt across the many black and white estates and other places in Singapore which resulted in the collection you see in this book. The image that kicked it all off, was taken at the Wessex Estate and it hangs in our living room today. When I called an end to my hunt, two years after it first started, my last photo session was in the Wessex Estate. Coincidentally therefore, my Black and White project started in the Wessex Estate and ended there.

In the short time that I have been in Singapore I have seen many green and open places being swallowed up by development projects necessary to keep pace with economic and social demands of a country with land constraints. Although the black and white houses are conservation properties, I do wonder whether their conservation extends to the landscapes that surround them. I have come across many a black and white house with condominiums built almost on top of them. Yes, the house has been retained but all of the surrounding landscape, that contribute to the look and the feel of the black and white house, has been lost. Perhaps, the landscapes that I have sought to capture in these images will also one day be lost to the juggernaut of growth. If that day comes, then my efforts might be a historical reminder of their glory. Of course, if this book inspires, promotes and enhances their continued conservation, together with their landscapes, then I will have truly achieved something special during my time in Singapore.

When speaking to the people, whose homes I was generously permitted to photograph, a common thread quickly appeared. Their choice in renting these black and white houses was, no doubt, a life style choice and they loved their homes, but they all felt the weight of the history of these houses and the generations that had preceded them. They said that as temporary guardians, charged with the momentary care for these homes, they wished for new stories and chapters to be added to their history. They knew they could never own these houses but, they each loved them as if they were their own. Their passion for these black and white houses made my project achievable.

This book would not have been possible without the support and encouragement shown by the many people who shared my story with their neighbours and indulged me with their own stories and experiences living in these homes. My experience in making this book, was all the more richer for the stories they shared with me. Their stories, in the context of the photos used in this book, are therefore now part of my story too.

I hope that you enjoy these landscapes of Singapore.

Peter Zaman

Singapore, July 2023.

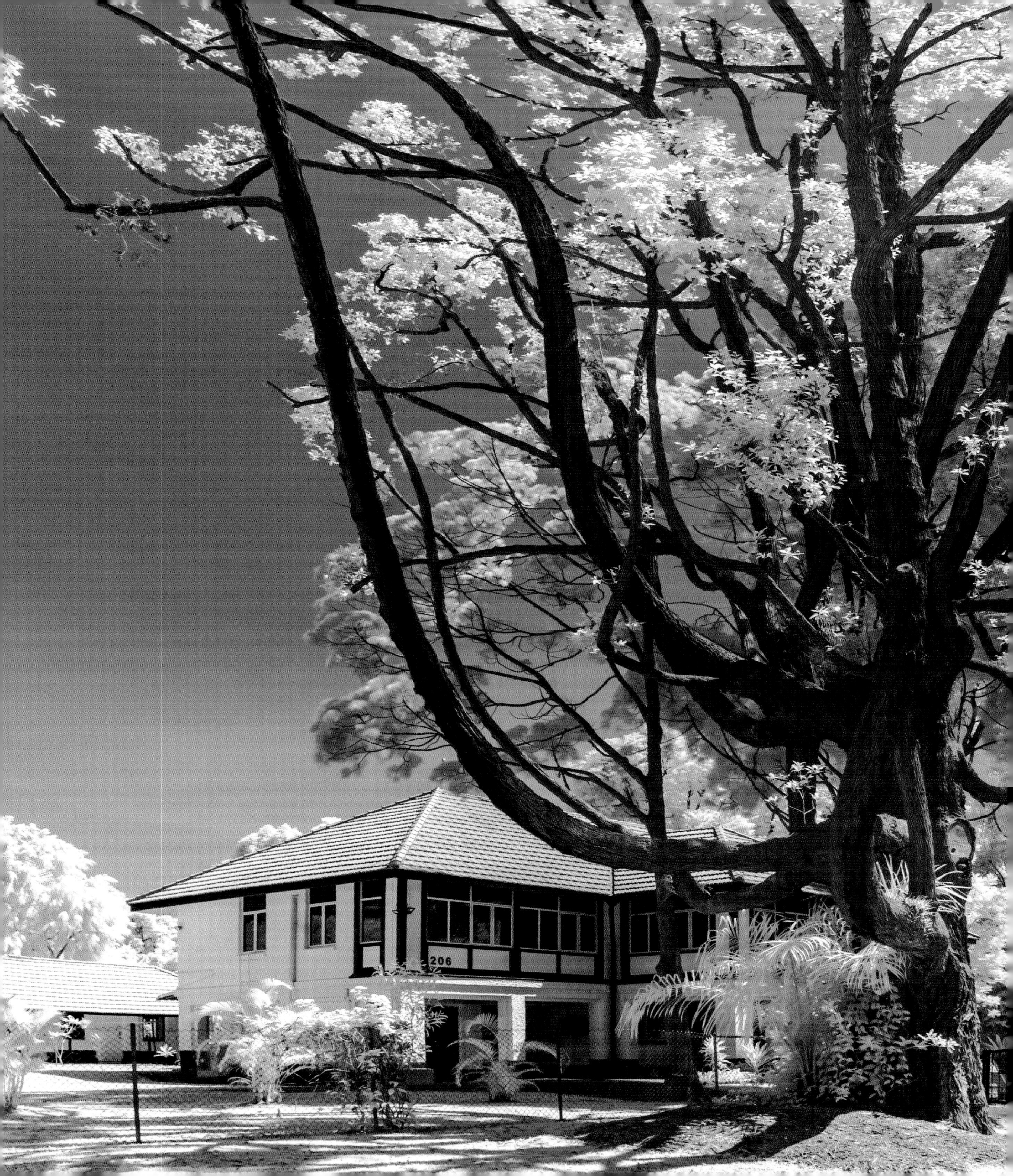
206

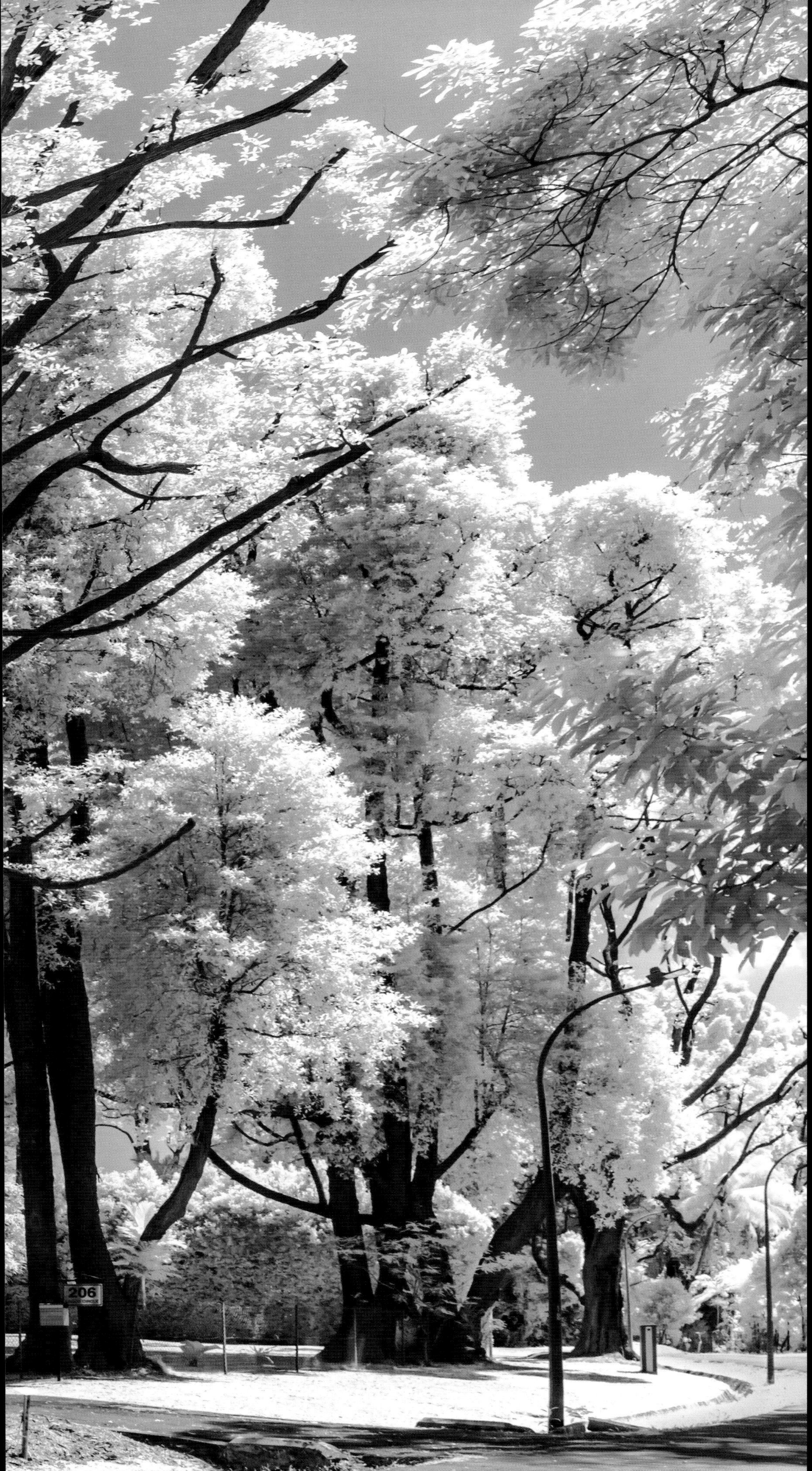

Cyrtophyllum fragrans, Tembusu

Black and white houses such as this one on Kay Siang Road were originally built to accommodate staff members of the Singapore Improvement Trust (SIT), forerunner of the Housing Development Board.

This particular house coincidentally was where Robert Davison, FRIBA, father of Dr Julian Davison, lived in the 1950s when it served as a mess for bachelor members of staff of the SIT. A few years later Robert Davison became a founding partner of the Singapore branch of the architectural firm Raglan Squire & Partners, which still exists today as RSP.

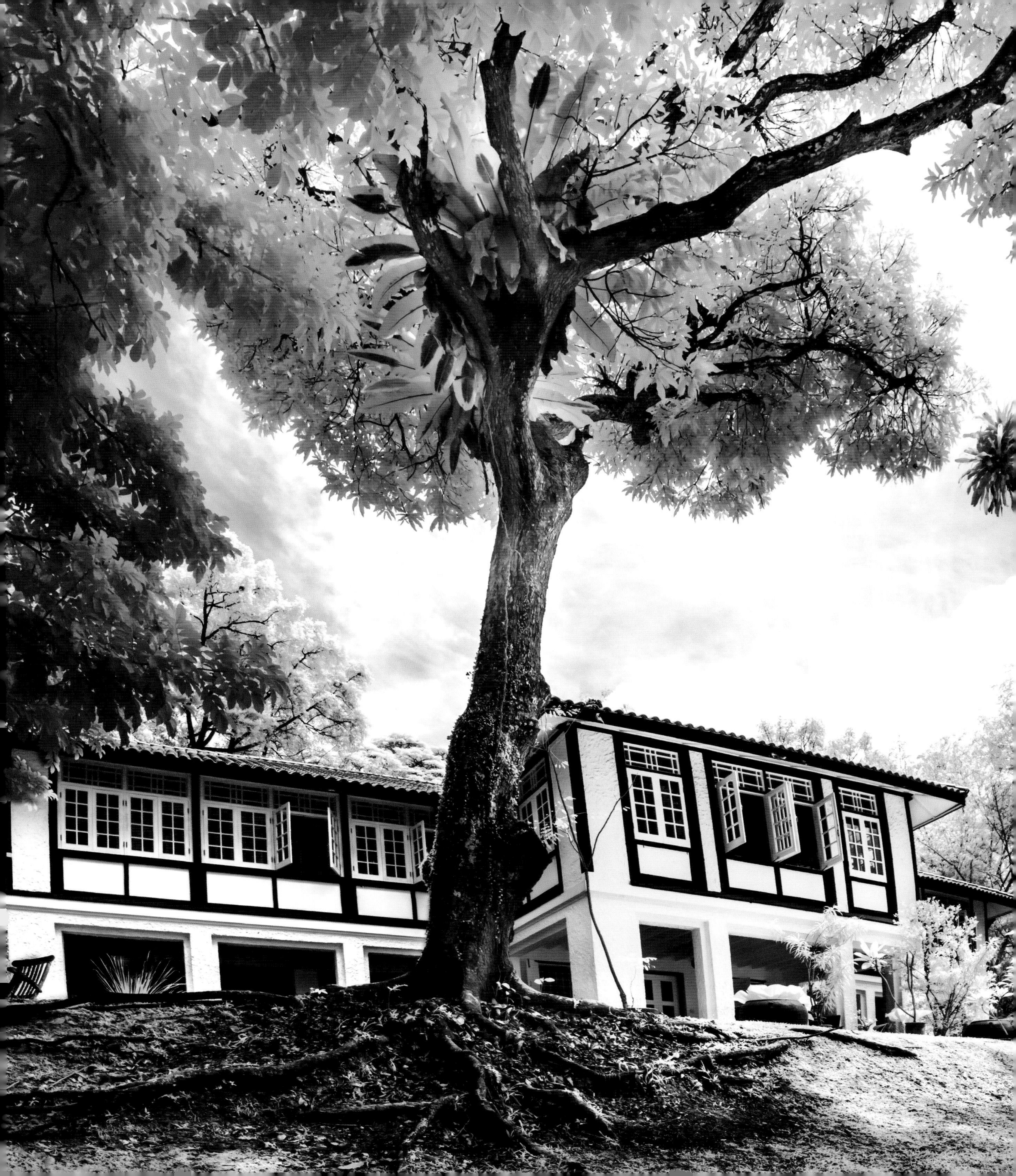

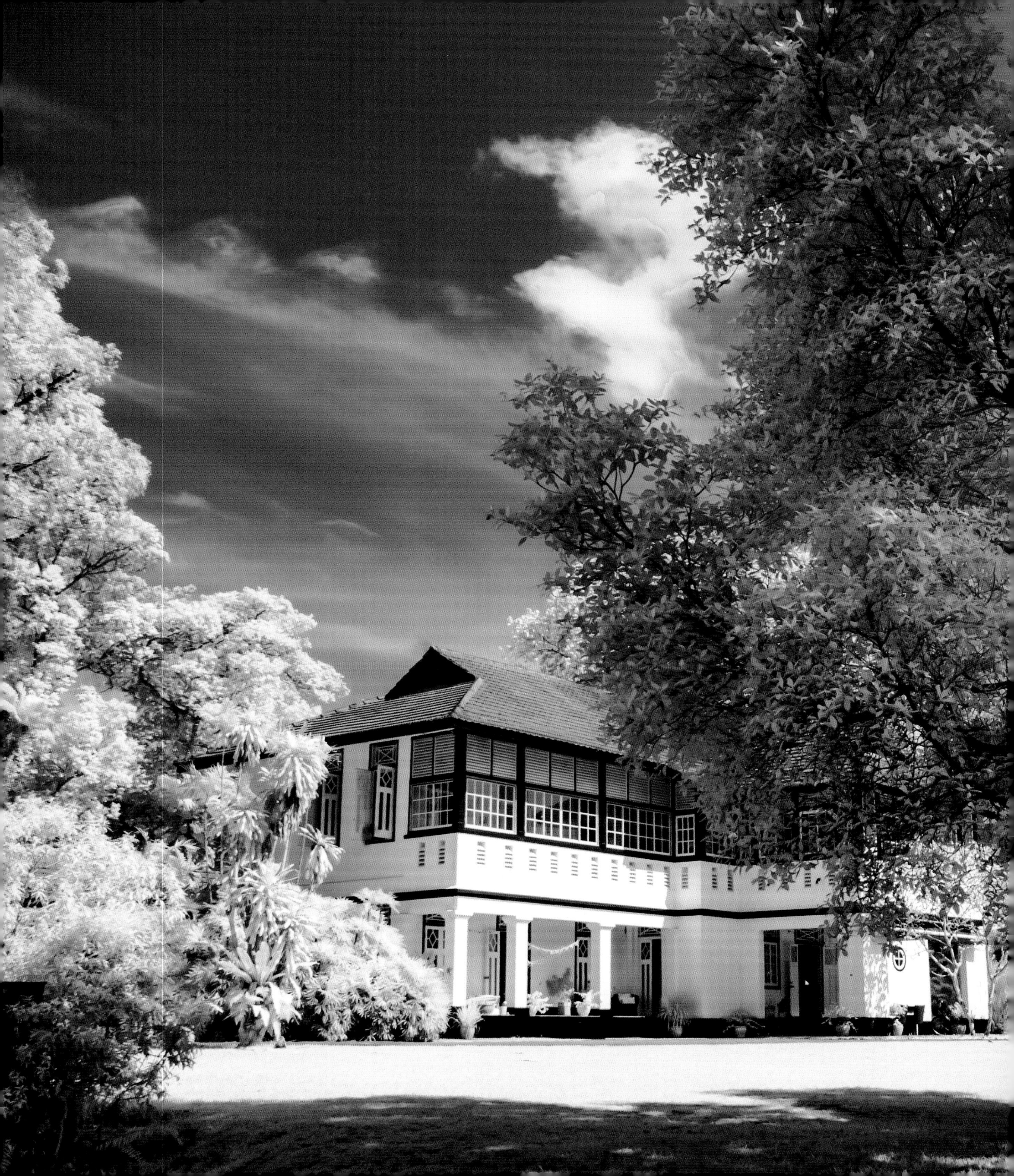

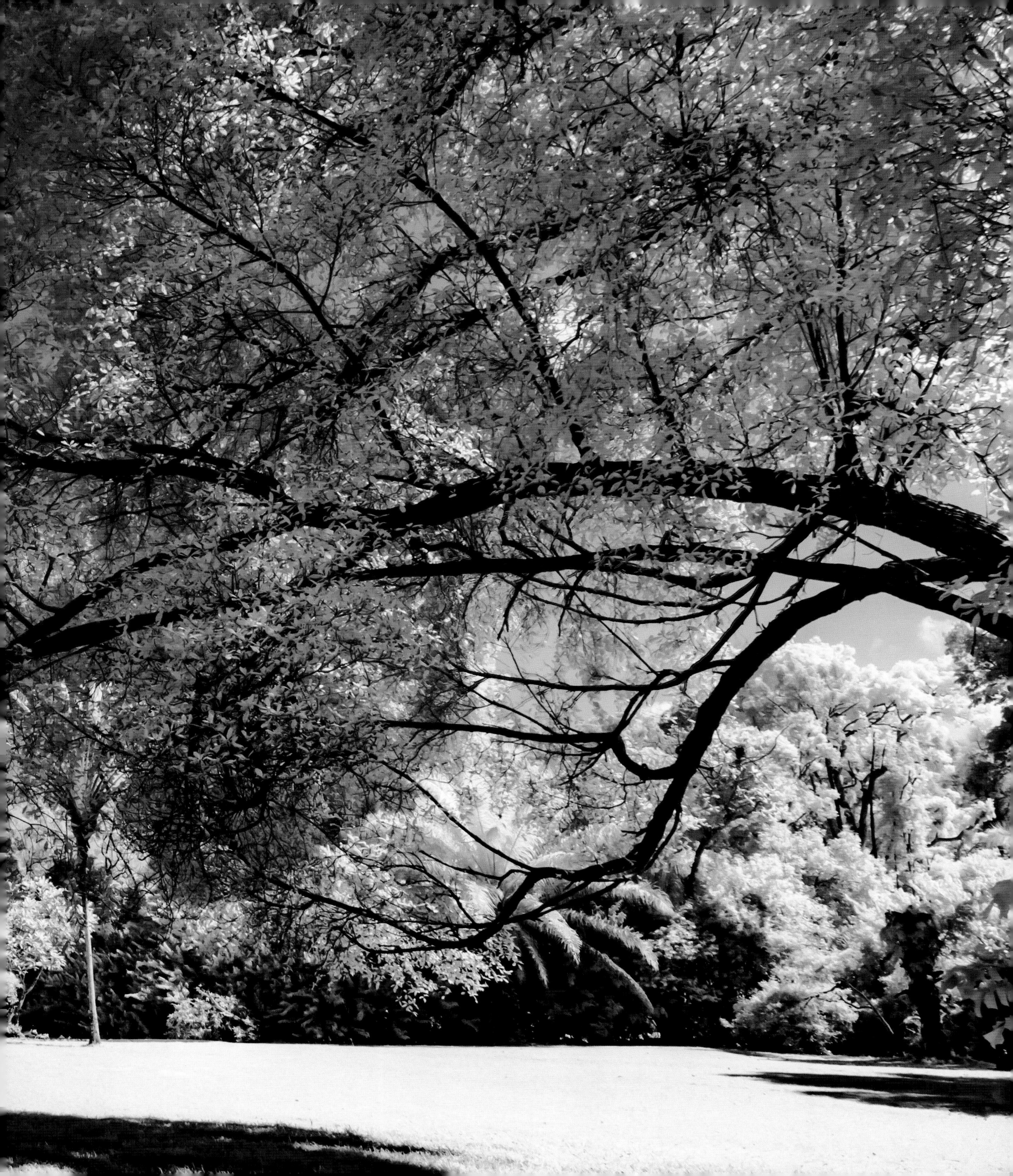

Seletar Camp, built in 1928 as the Royal Air Force's main base in the Far East, at some point housed 2000 RAF personnel and their families.

In 'Seleterville', as it was affectionately called then, the roads are named after London Underground Stations such as Park Lane, Edgware Road and Maida Vale.

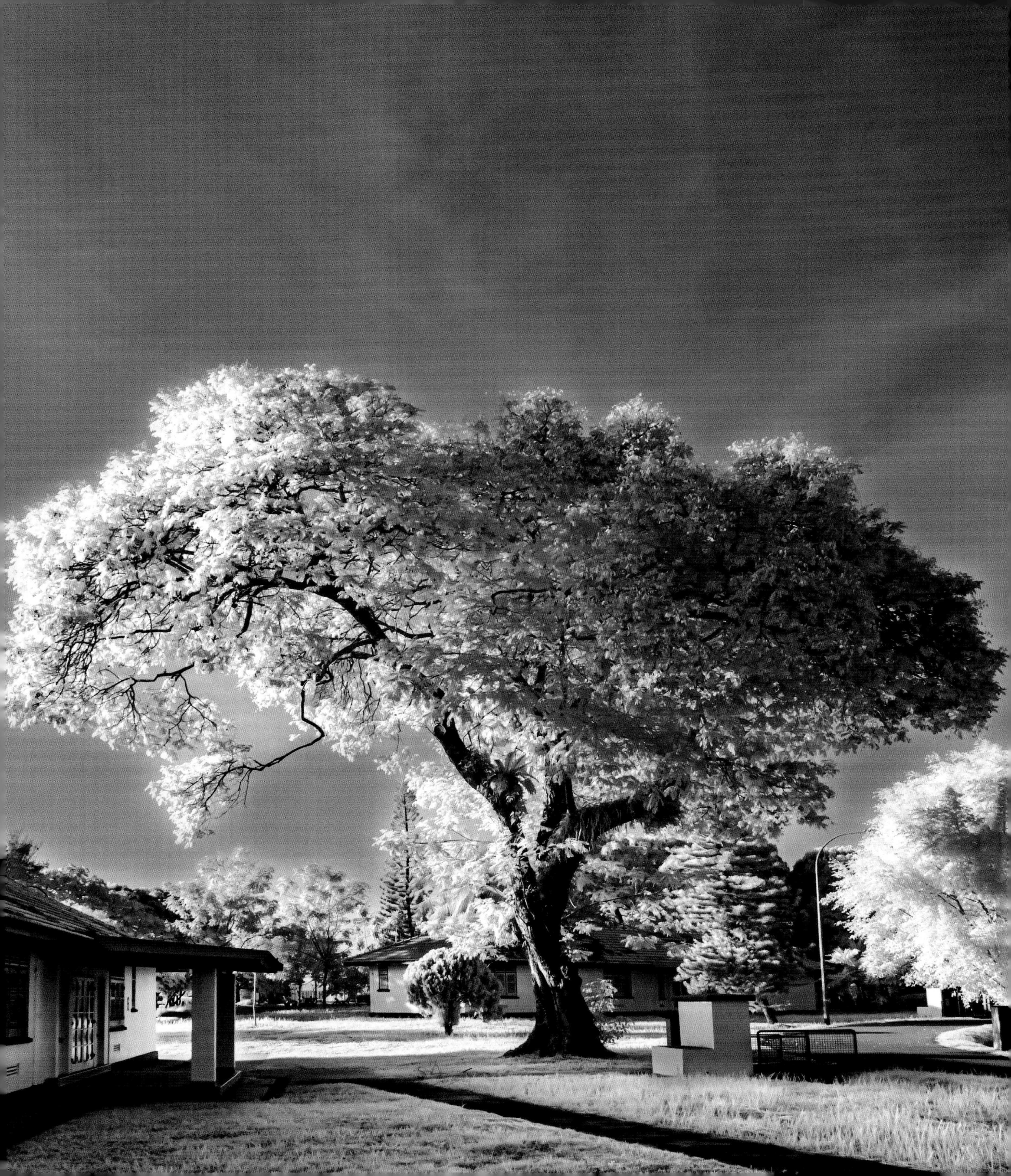

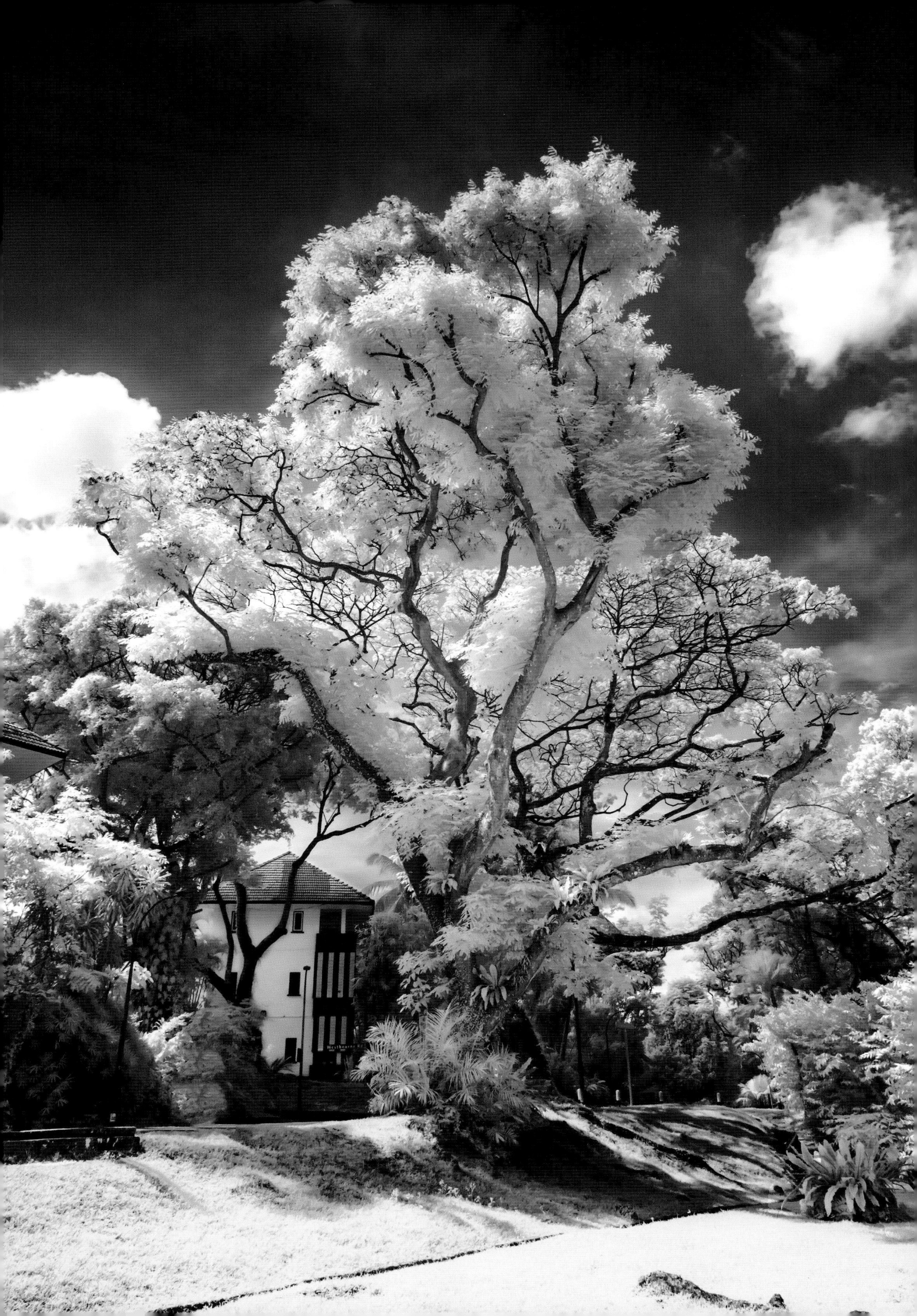
Westbourne Rd

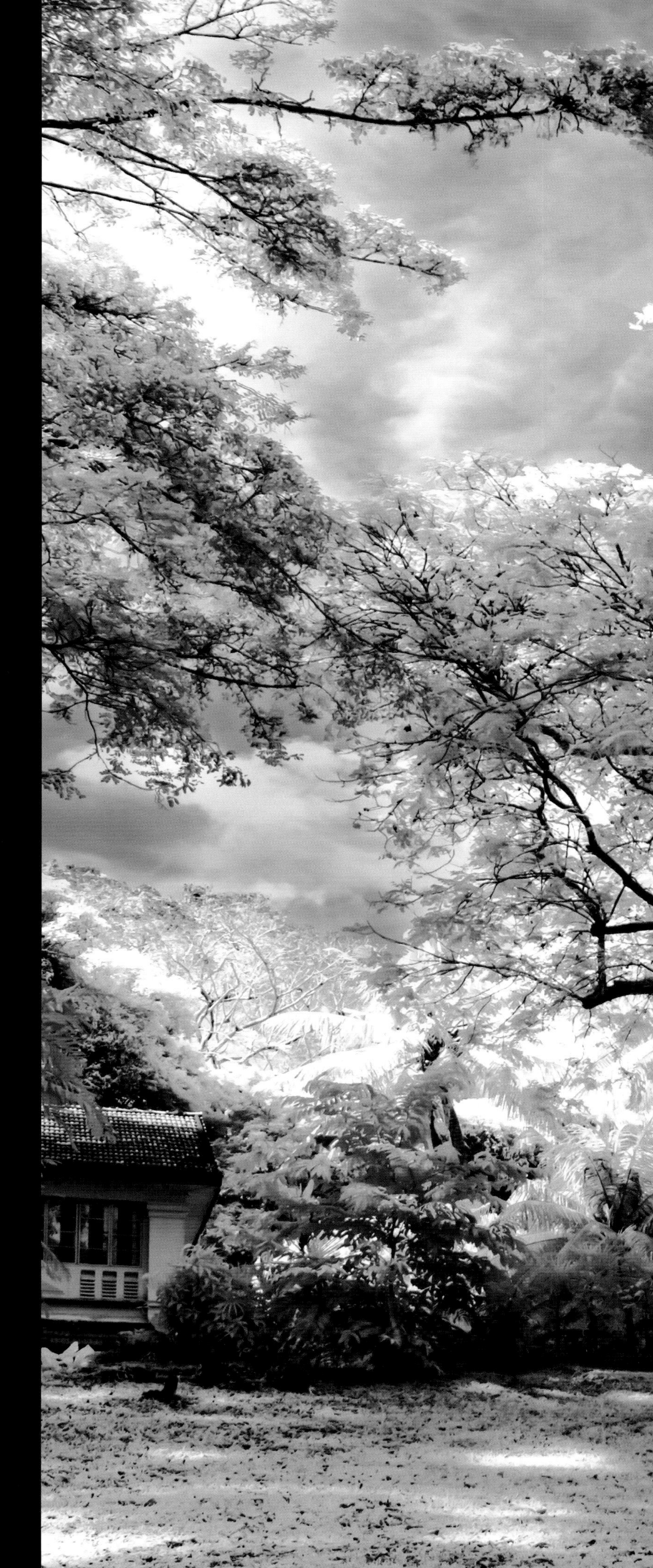

Samanea saman, Rain Tree

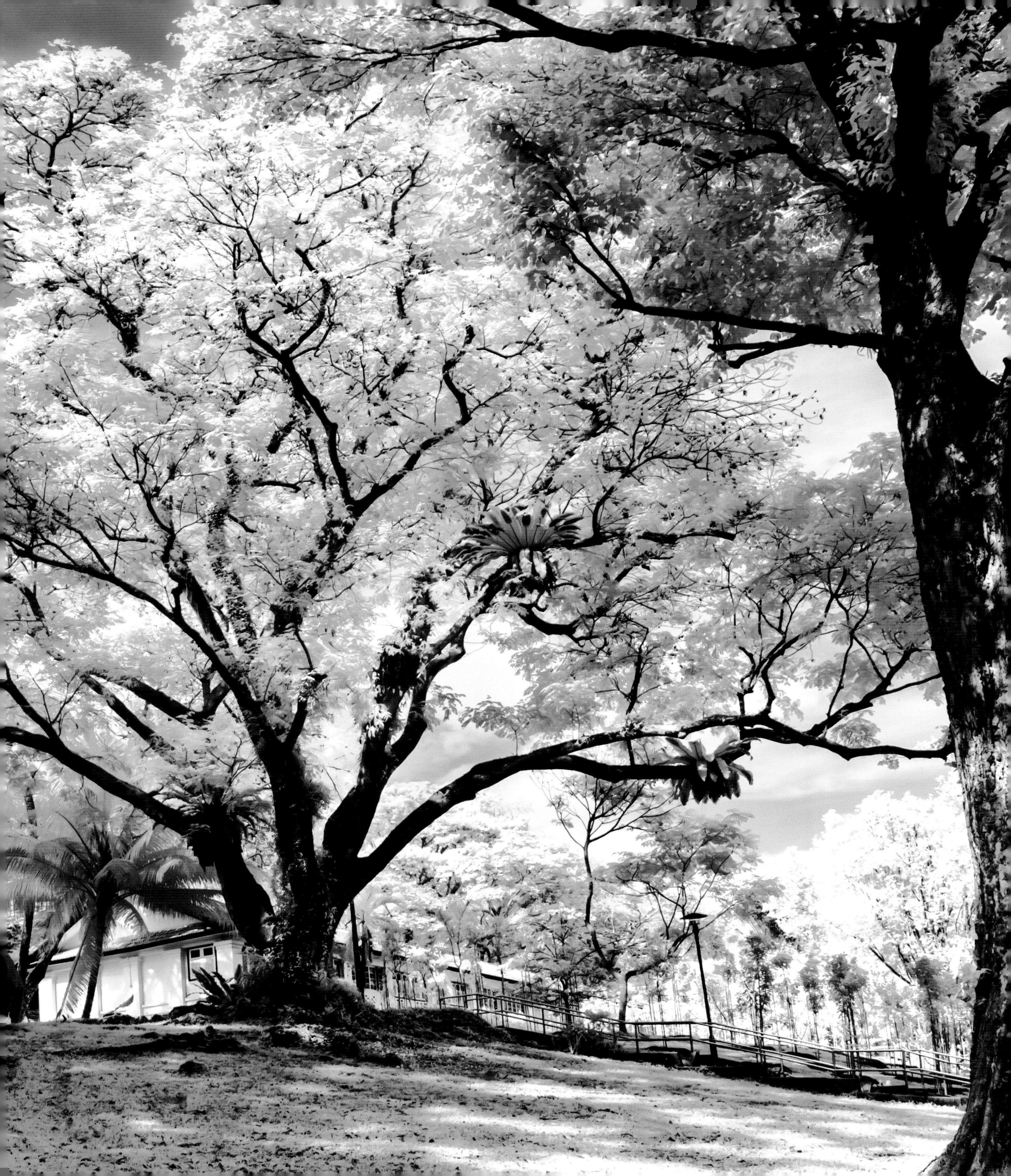

This tree is called Cook's Pine because Europeans first learned about it after Captain James Cook's voyage to New Caledonia. It has a curious characteristic; no matter where it grows the entire tree leans, from the base to the crown, towards the equator. This is unique among all the trees in the world.

Source: Johns, J. W., J. M. Yost, D. Nicolle, B. Igic, and M. K. Ritter. 2017. Worldwide hemisphere-dependent lean in Cook pines. Ecology 98(9):2482–2484.

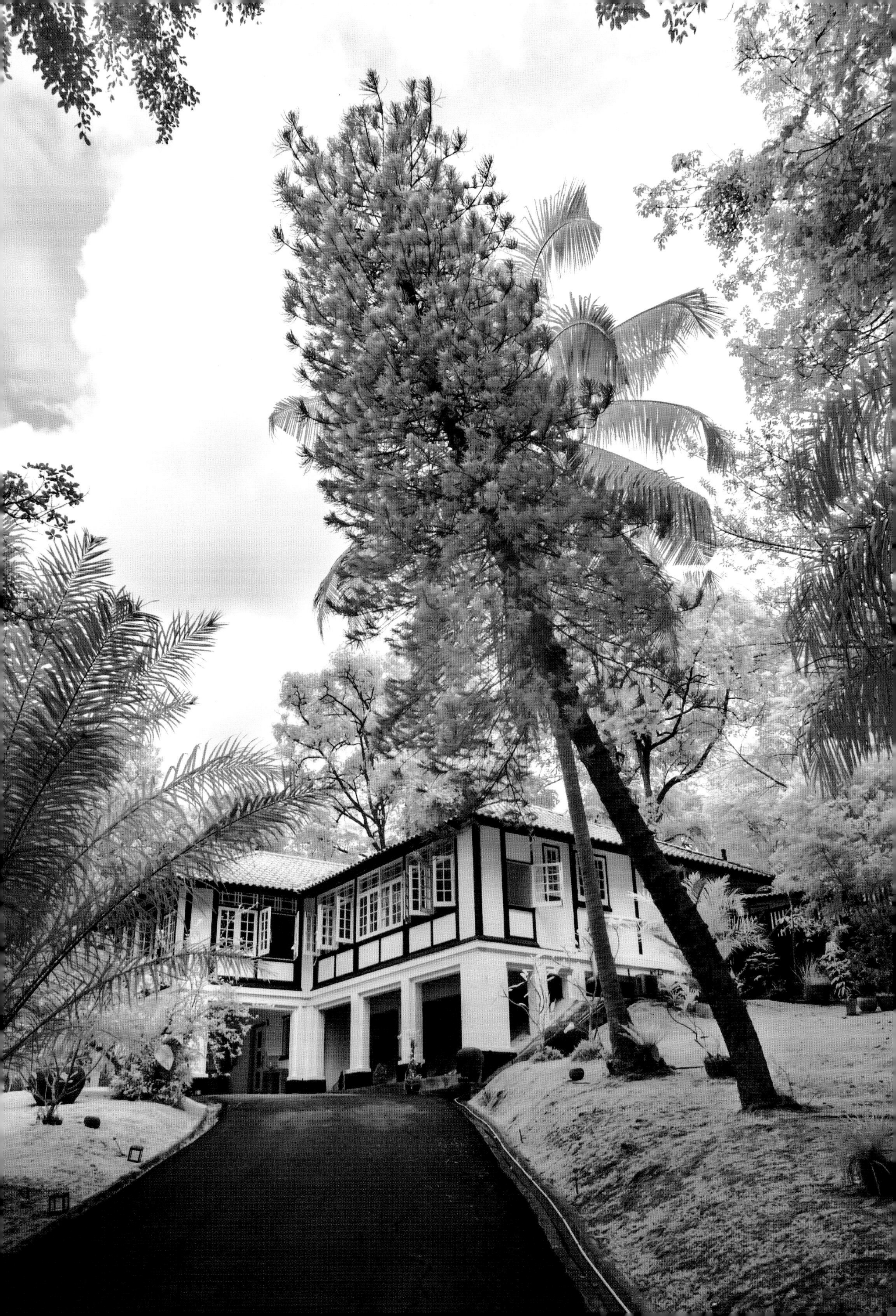

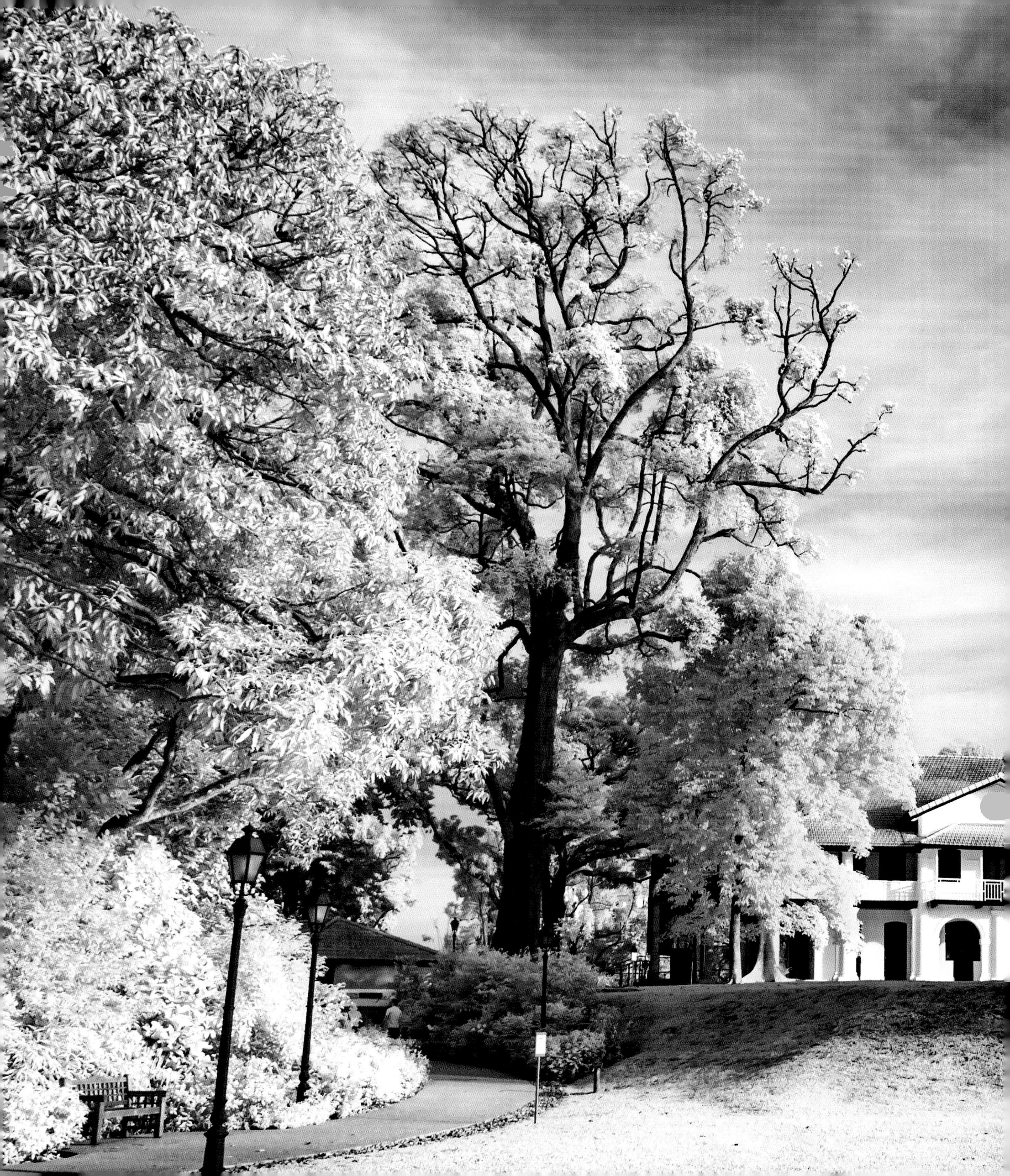

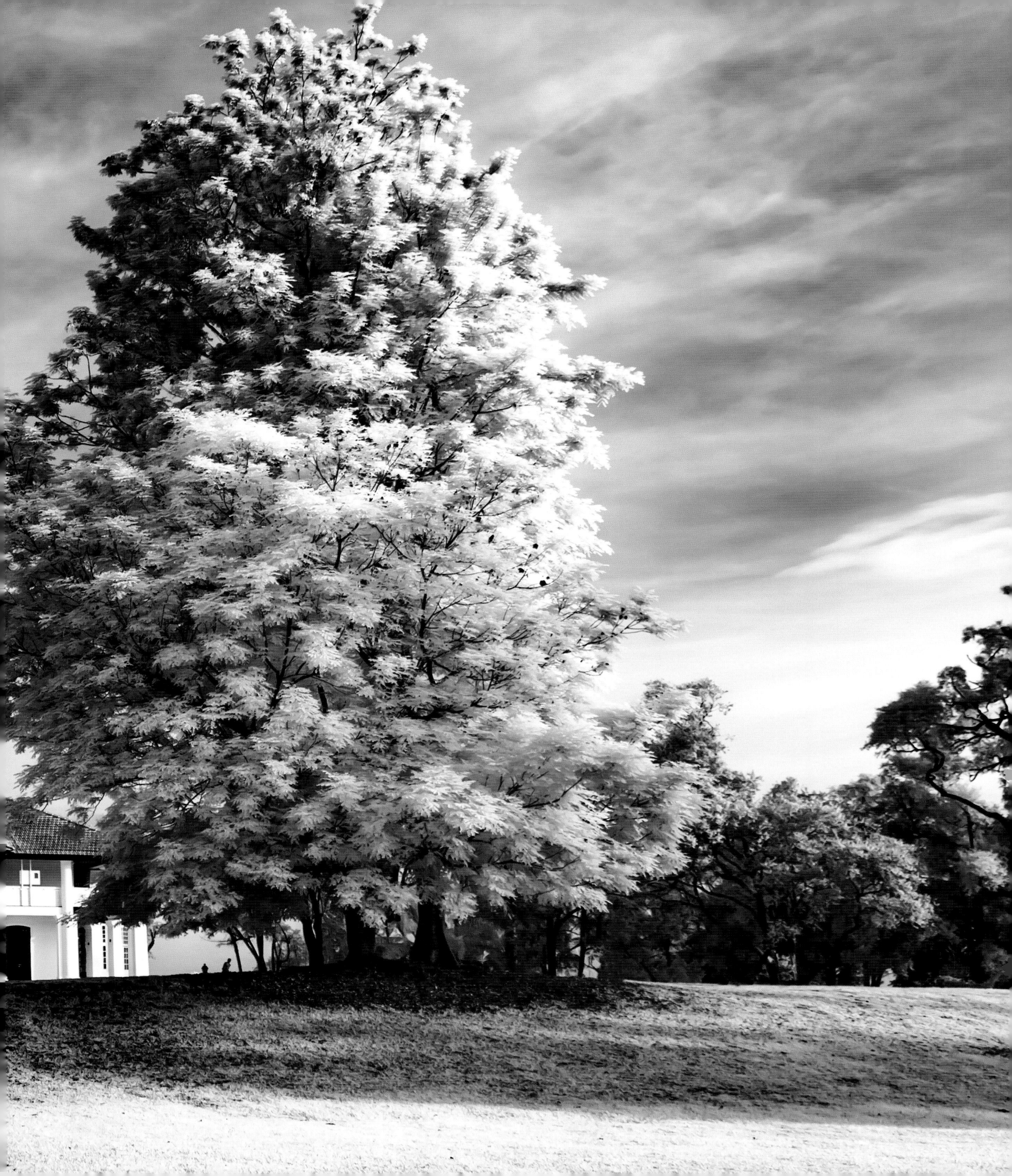

The bungalows at Pender Road were built for officers of the Eastern Extension Telegraph Company, and were designed by Swan & Mclaren between 1908-19.

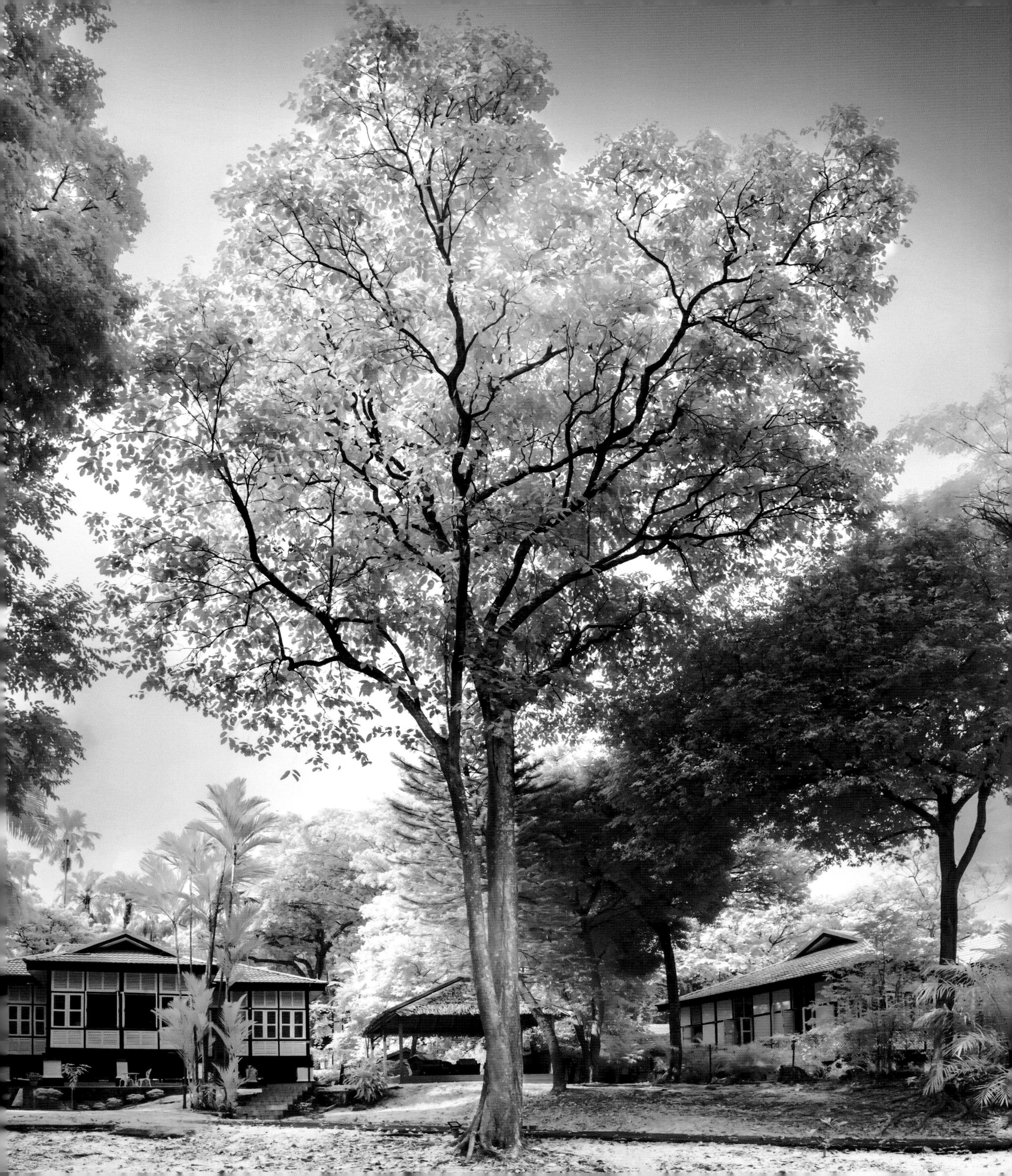

What I love the most about the Rain Trees are its branches. They twist and turn, sometimes upon themselves as if wrestling, climbing all the time to reach the light.

When you come across a road lined with Rain Trees on either side, it really is special. As you pass through, the rays of sunlight creep through gaps in the canopy creating an almost ethereal play of light and shadow. It transports you to a bygone era, where nature once-ruled our world.

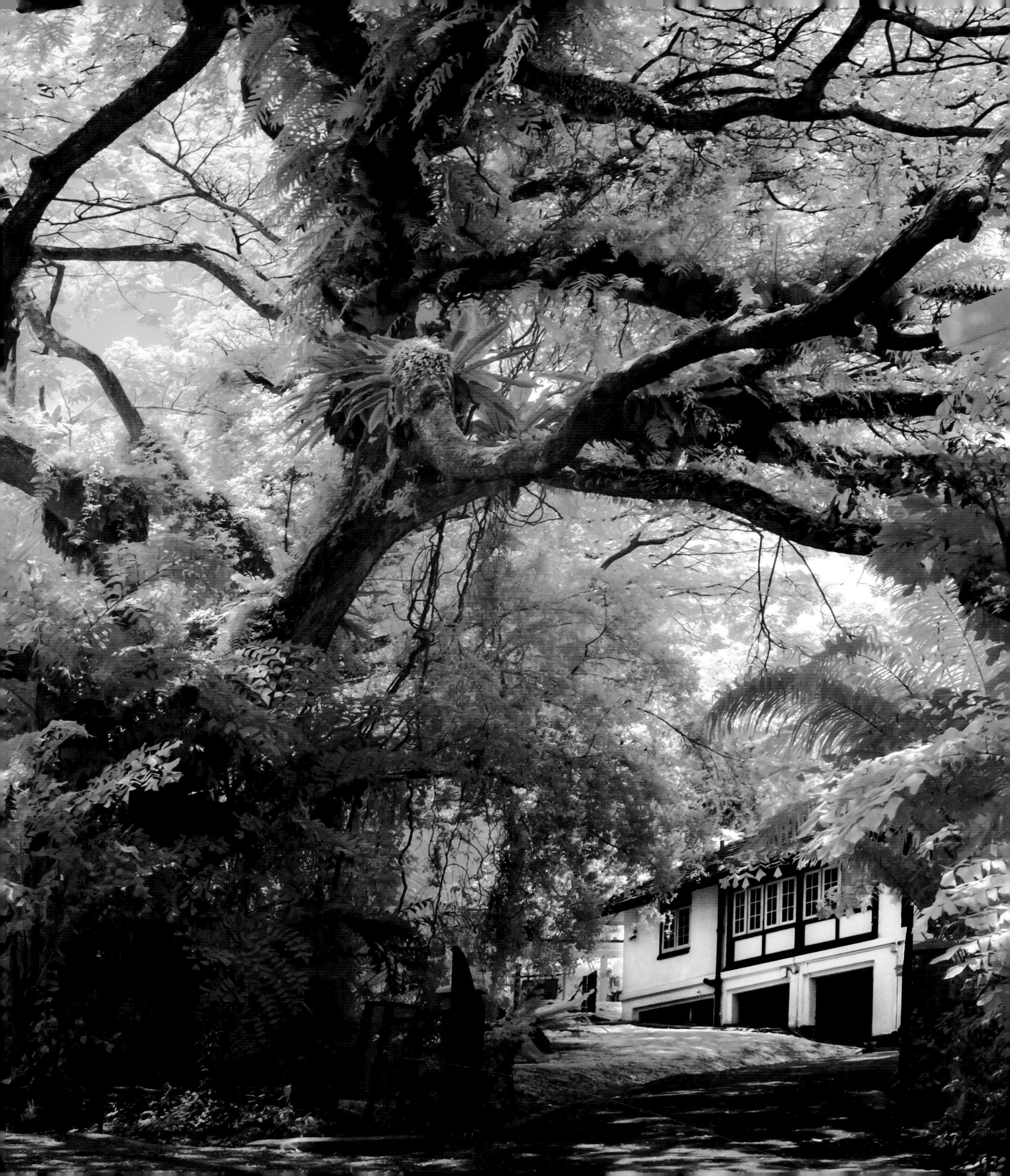

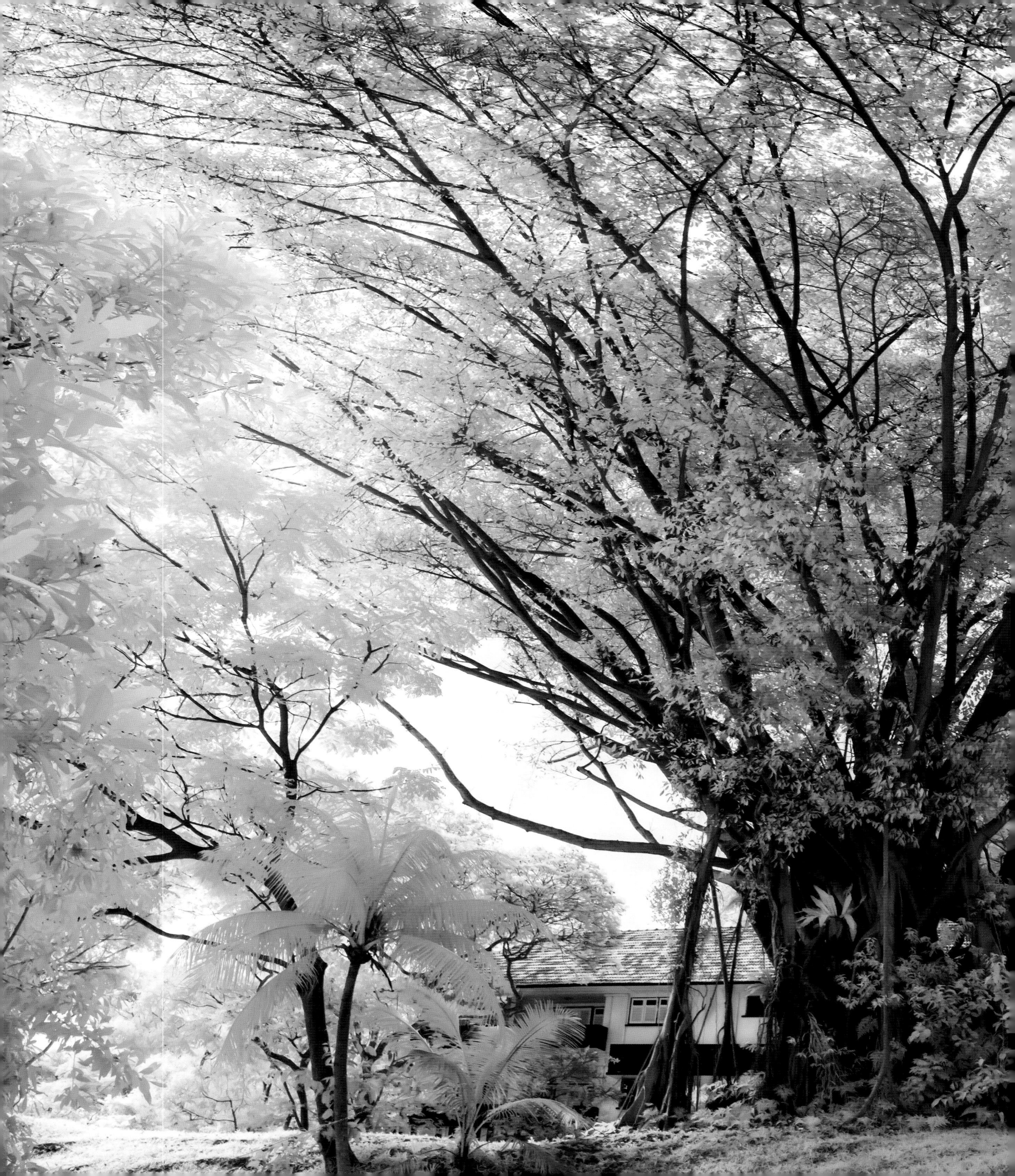

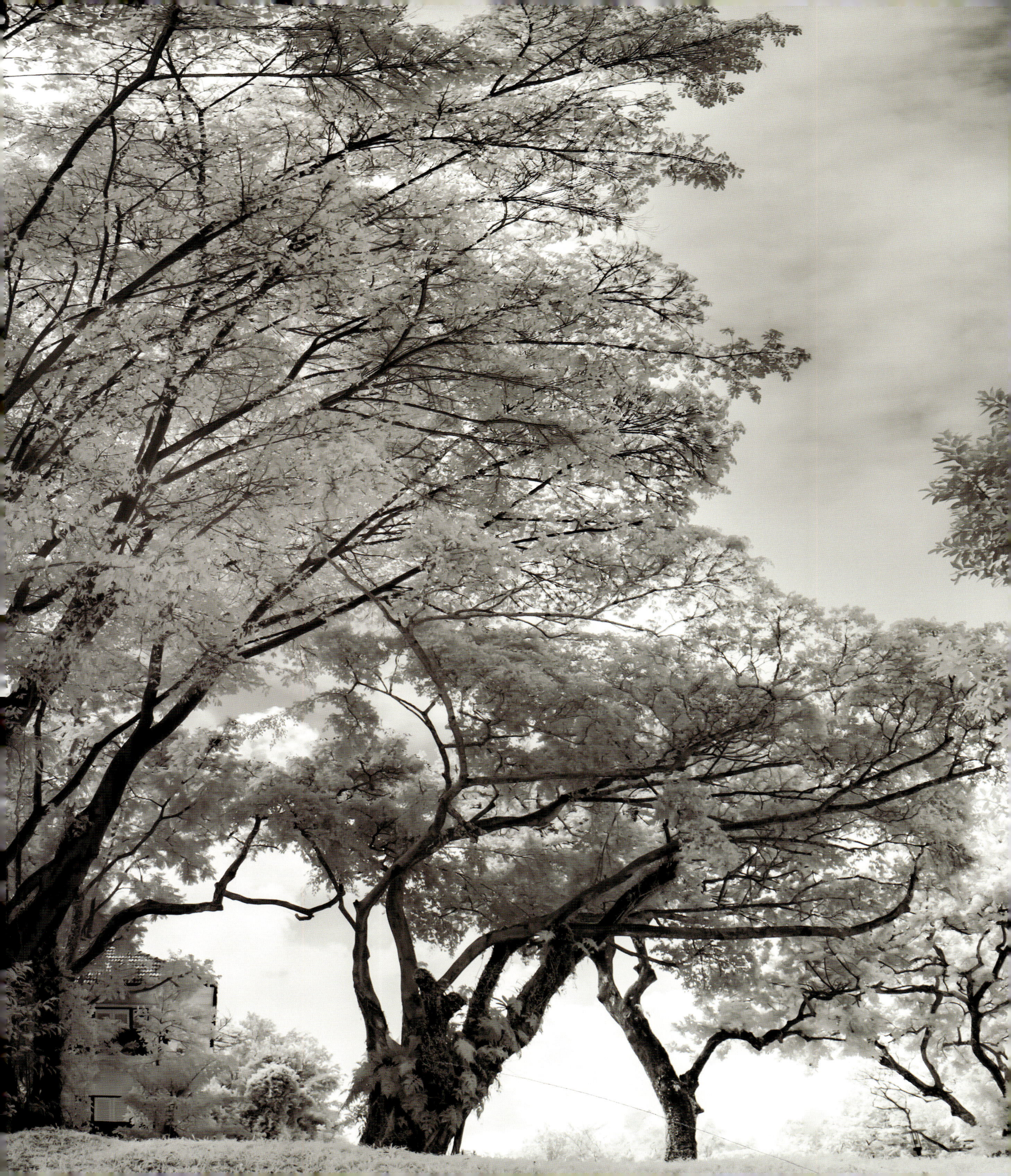

"I think I have learnt something of the value of stillness. I don't fret so much; I laugh at myself more often; I don't laugh at others. I live life at my own pace. Like a banyan tree. Is this wisdom, or is it just old age?"

- Ruskin Bond, A Book of Simple Living : Brief Notes from the Hills

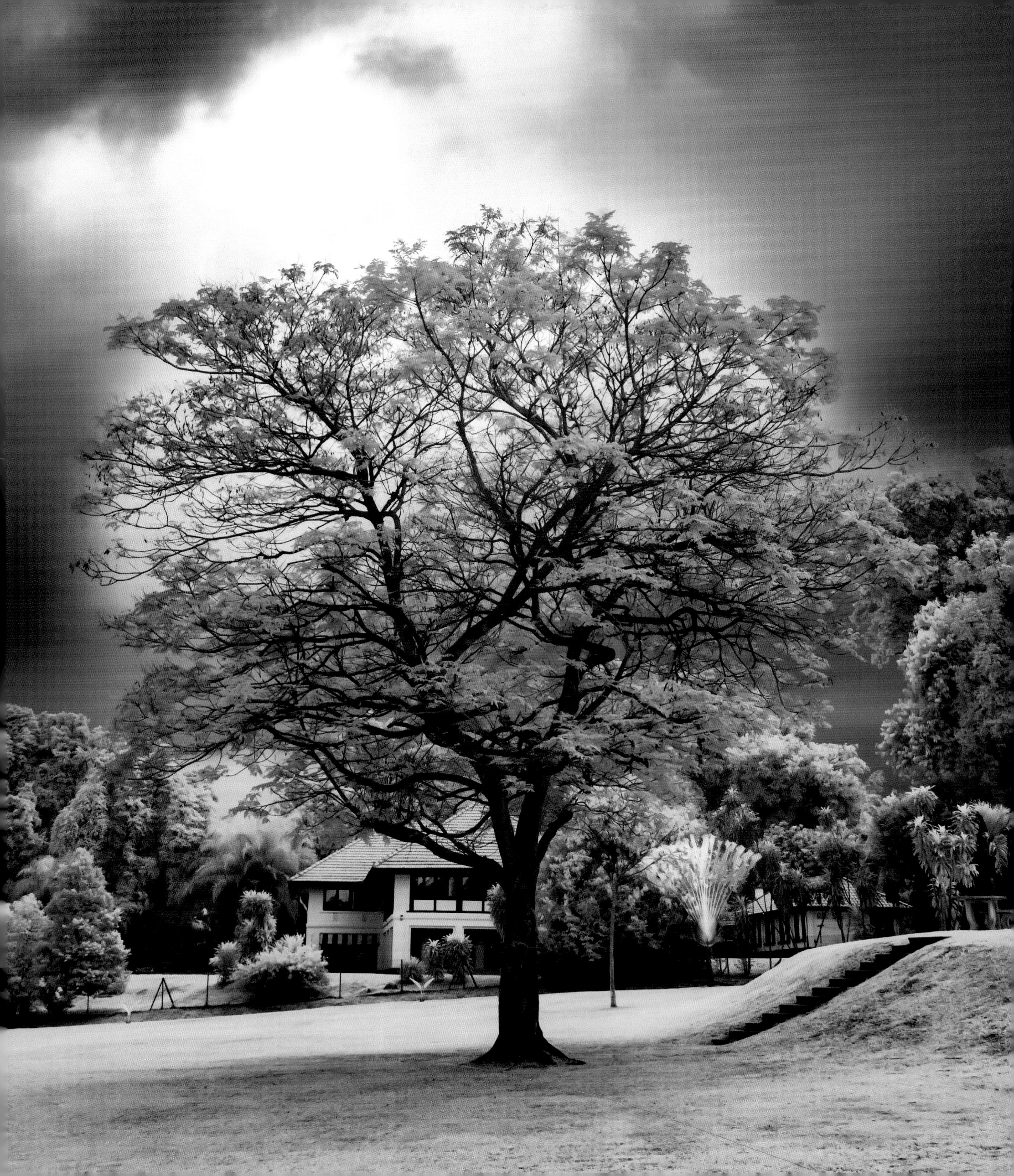

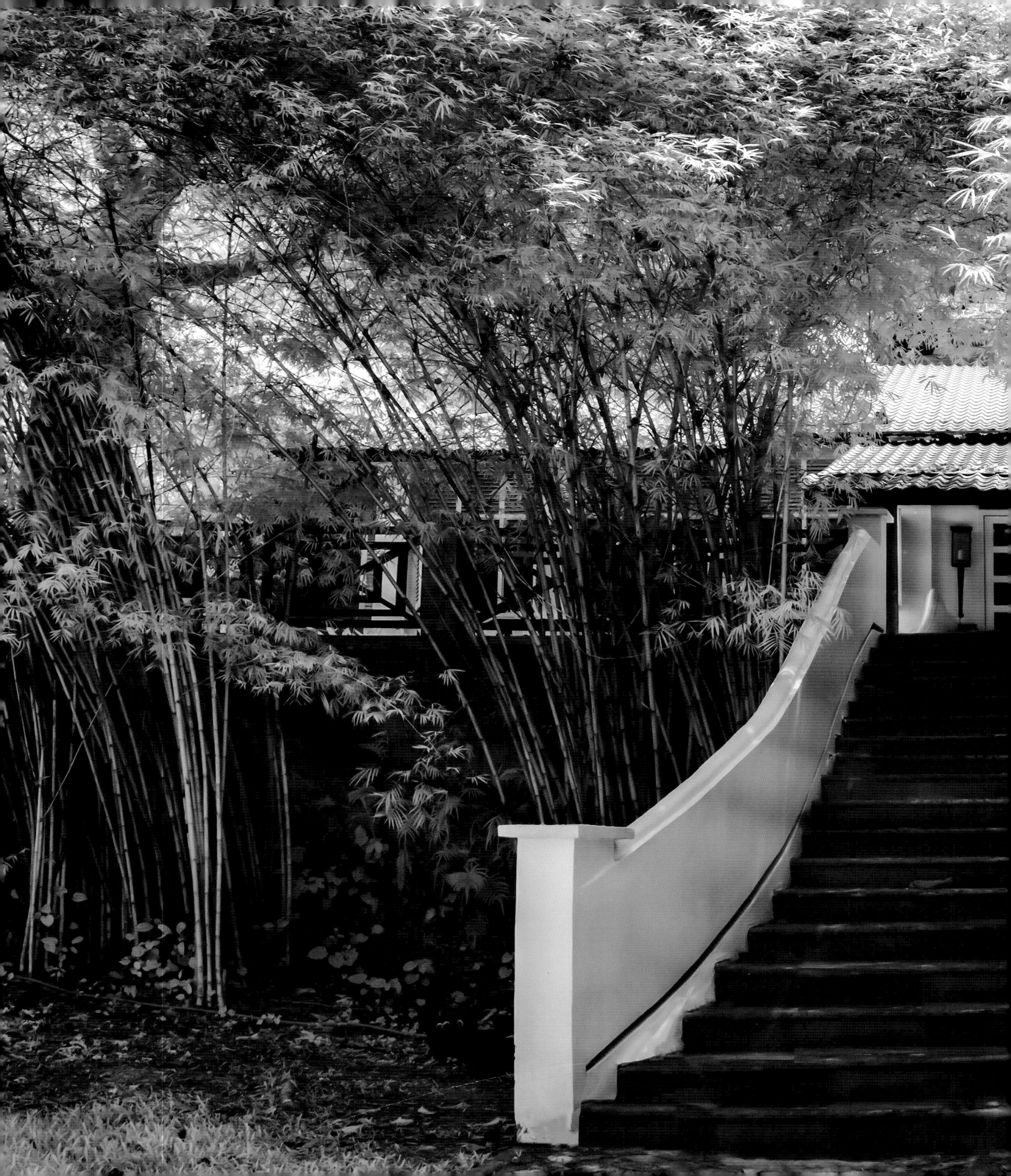

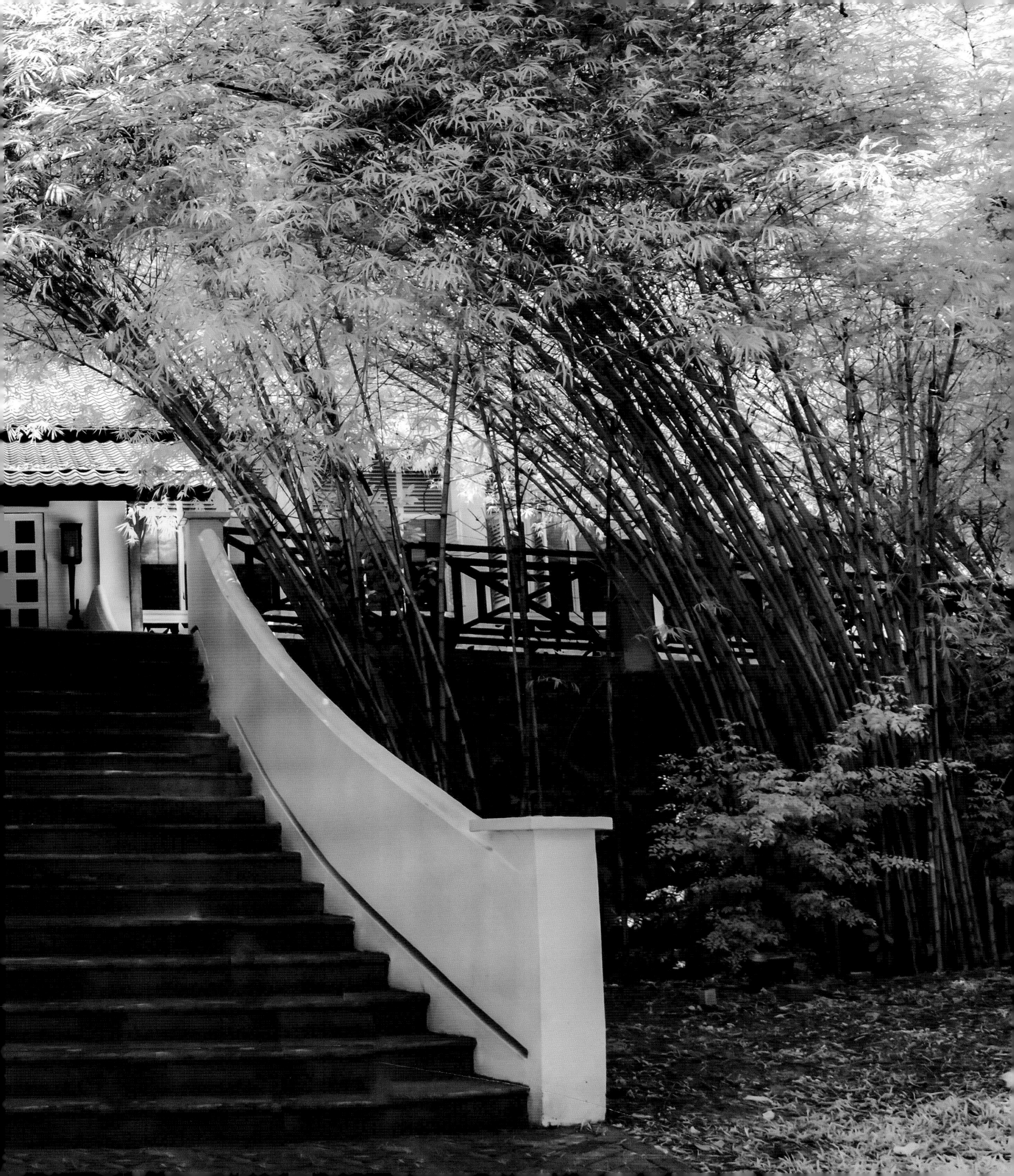

On Winchester Road, one feature of the black and white house is their positioning on the side of the slope, with the front elevation of the house raised on bricks or concrete piers and the rear of the house at ground level.

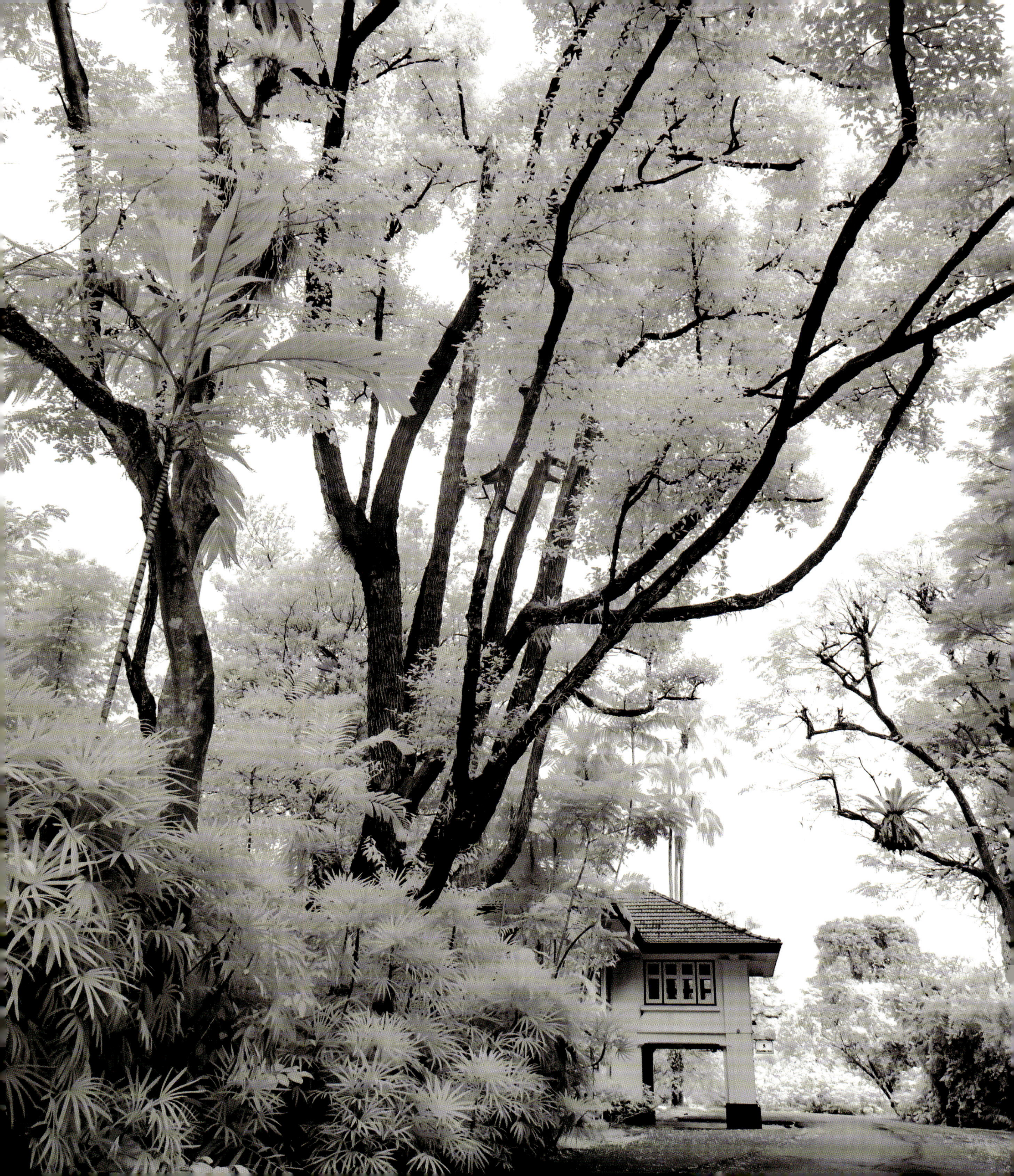

Singapore may be a small country but there are surprises waiting to be found.

Because of the way they are set back from the road, sometimes down a slope, the black and white houses in Malcolm Park are hard to photograph from the main road.

One of my Singapore surprises was finding this hidden green space, where I could photograph a Malcolm Park house from the back. The green space itself was amazing, the chance to photograph a black and white, a bonus.

 Acacia cincinnata, Scorpion Wattle

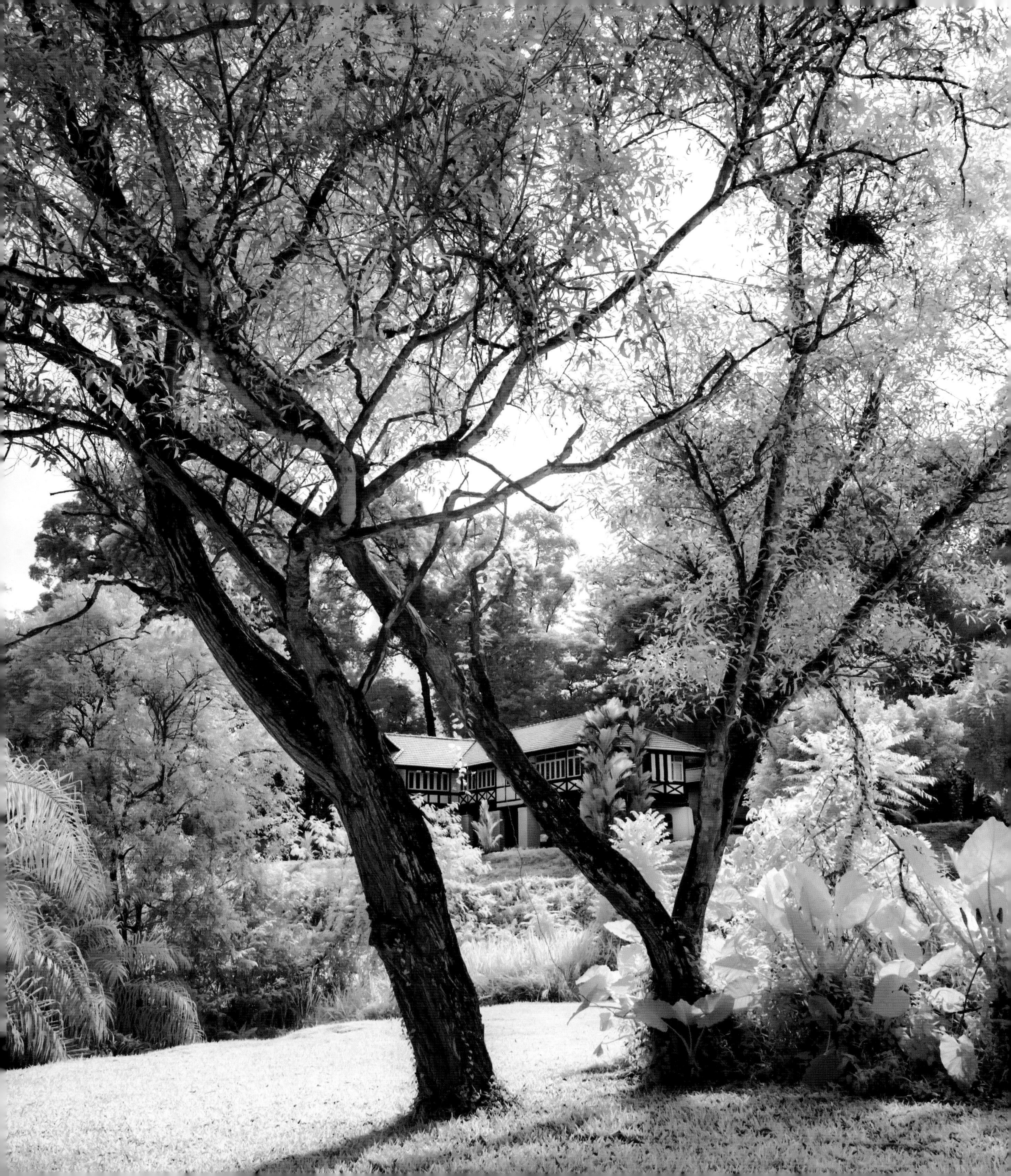

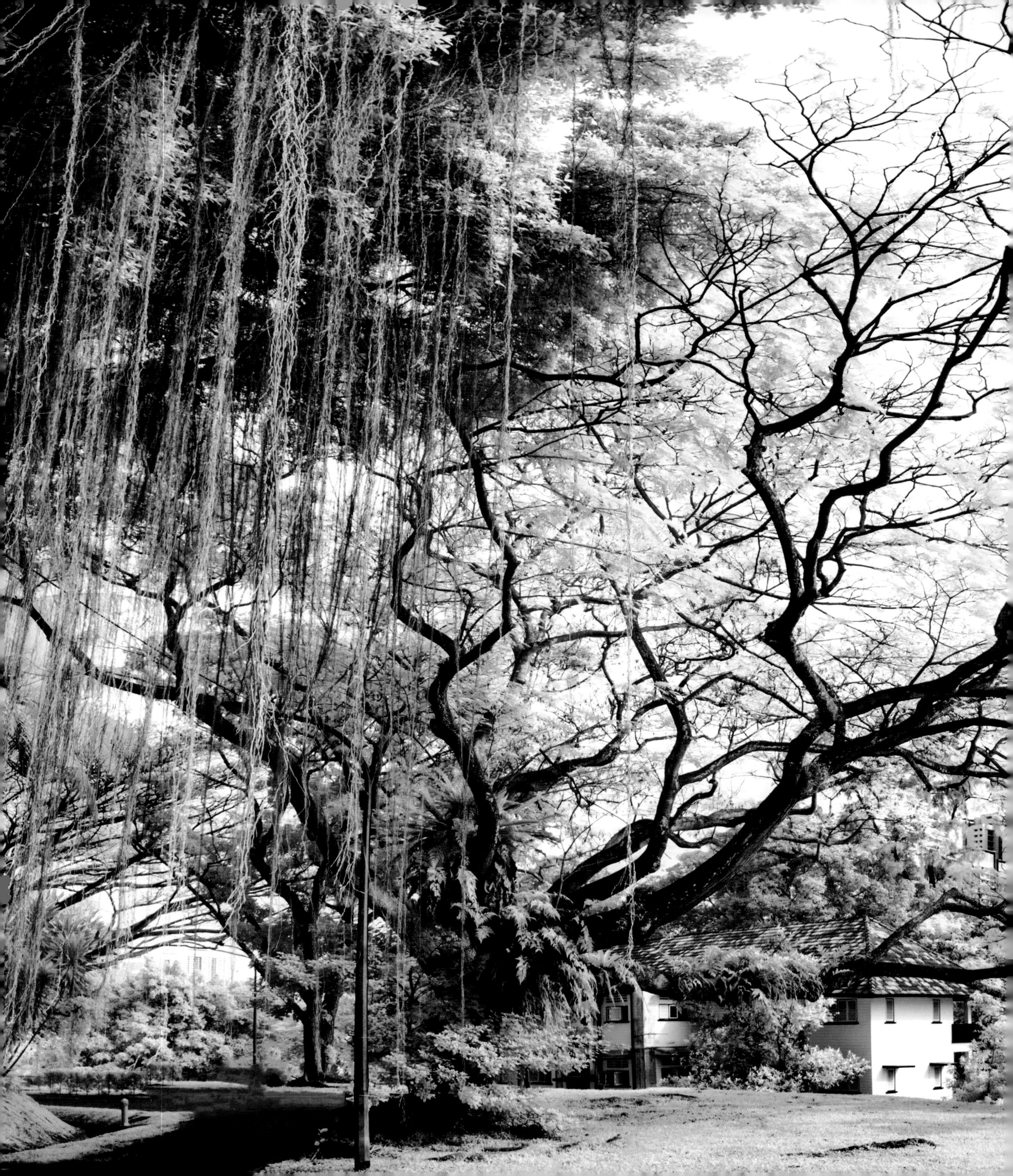

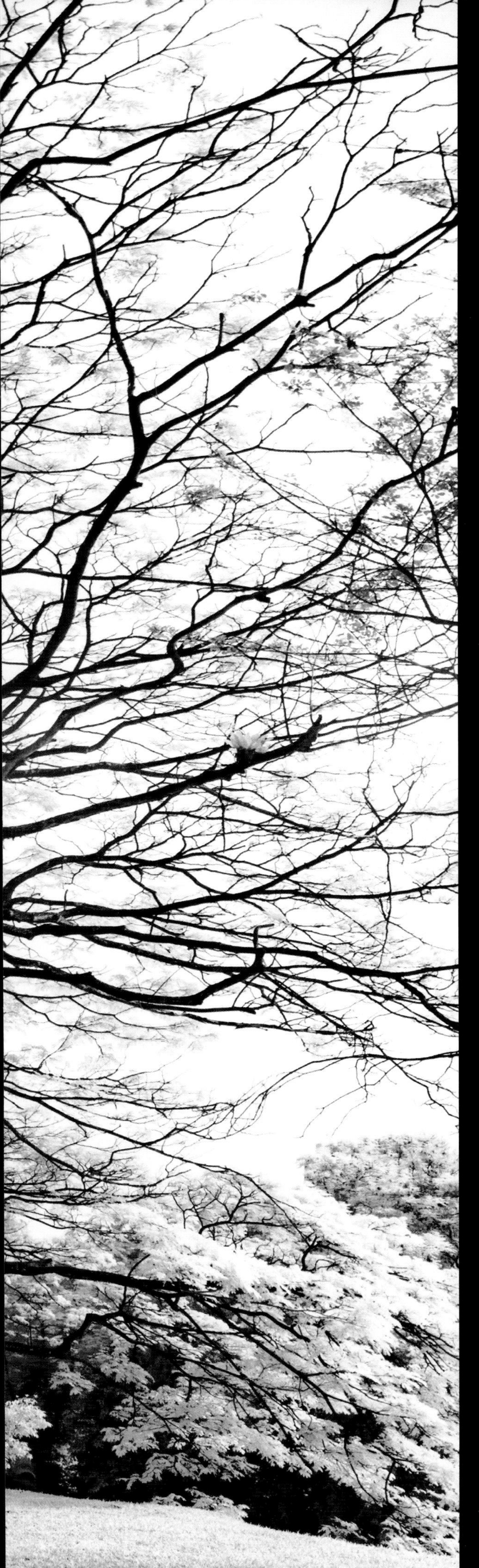

Samanea saman, Rain Tree

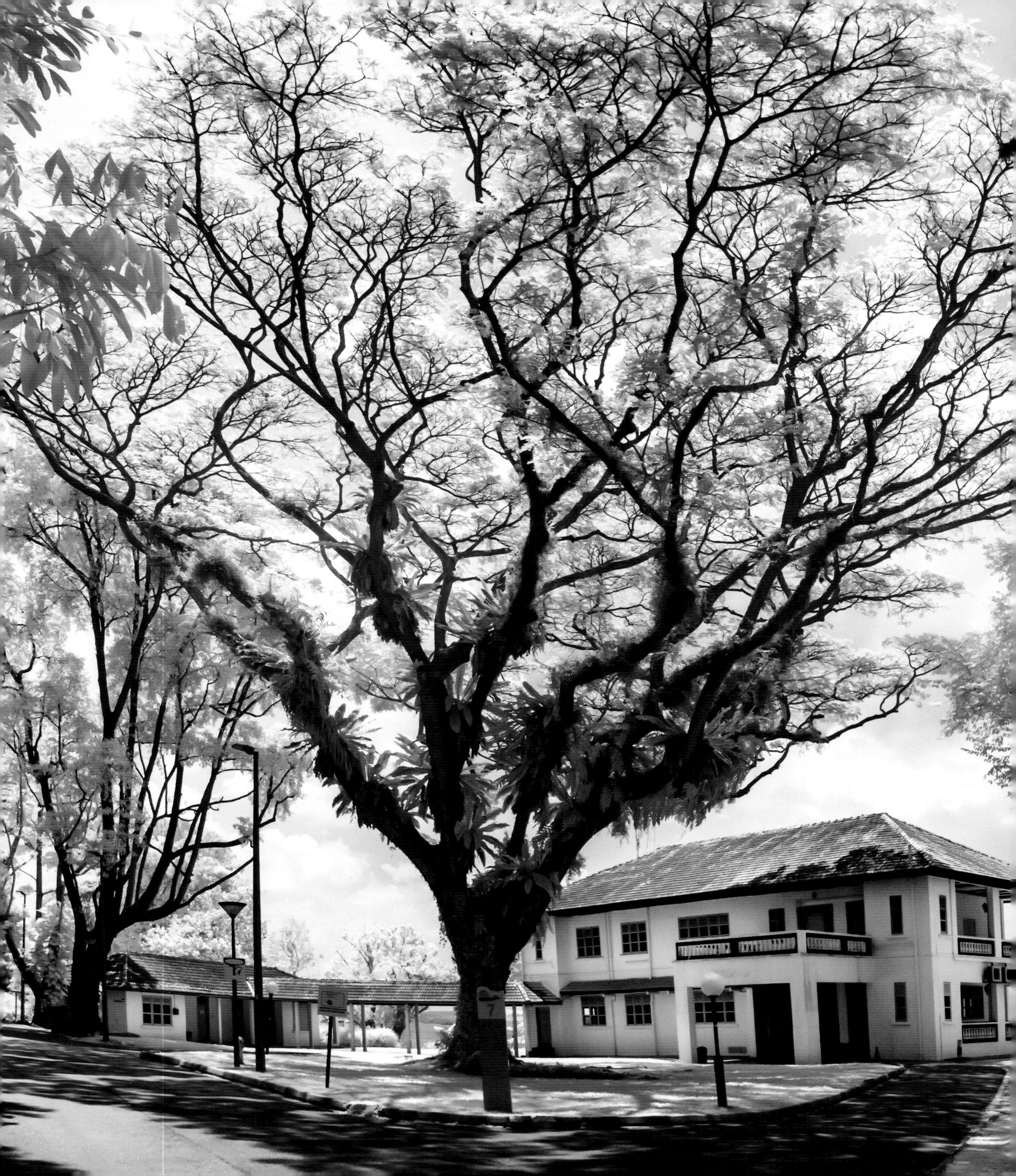
7

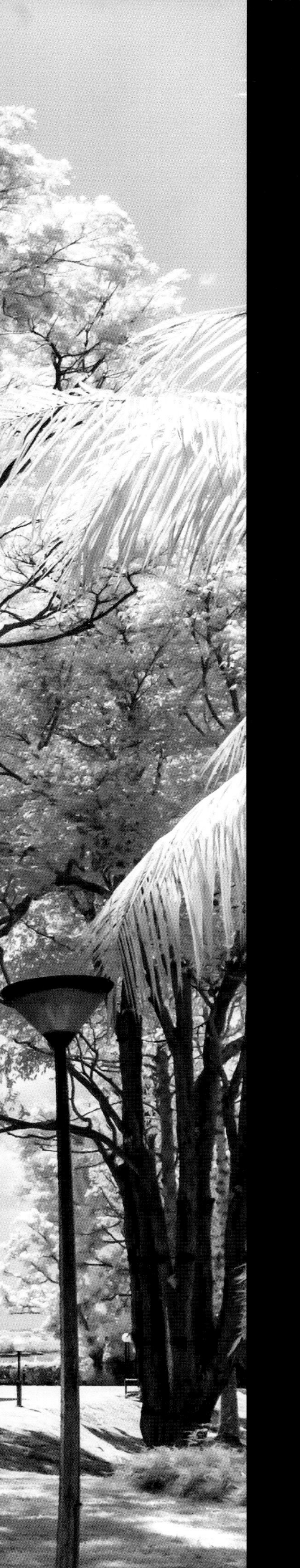

"Gymkhana: a meet featuring sports contests or athletic skills: such as competitive games on horseback"*

Today, Gymkhana Road leads to the Riding Academy at the Singapore Polo Club. Is this just coincidence?

*Miriam-Webster Dictionary

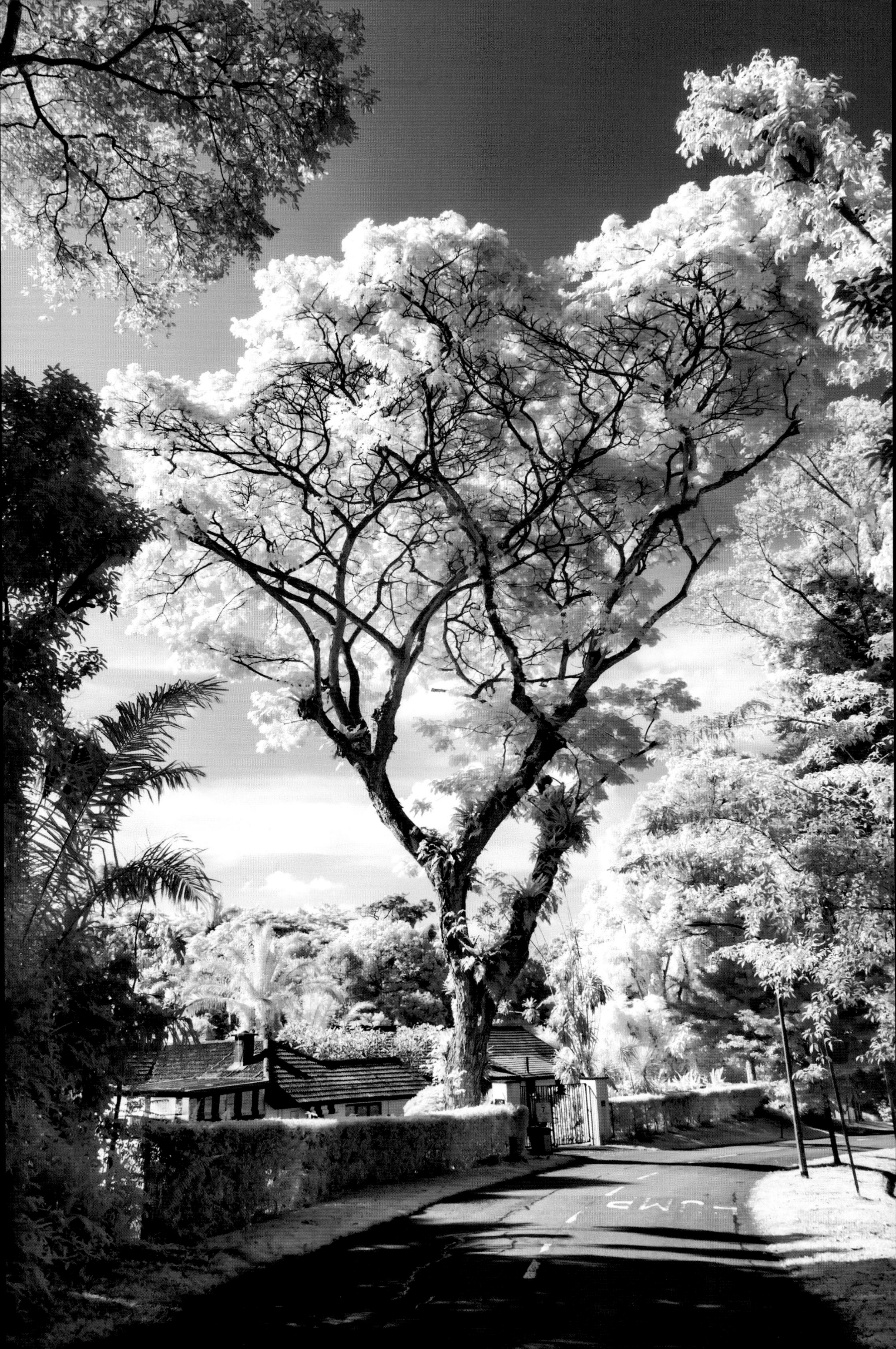

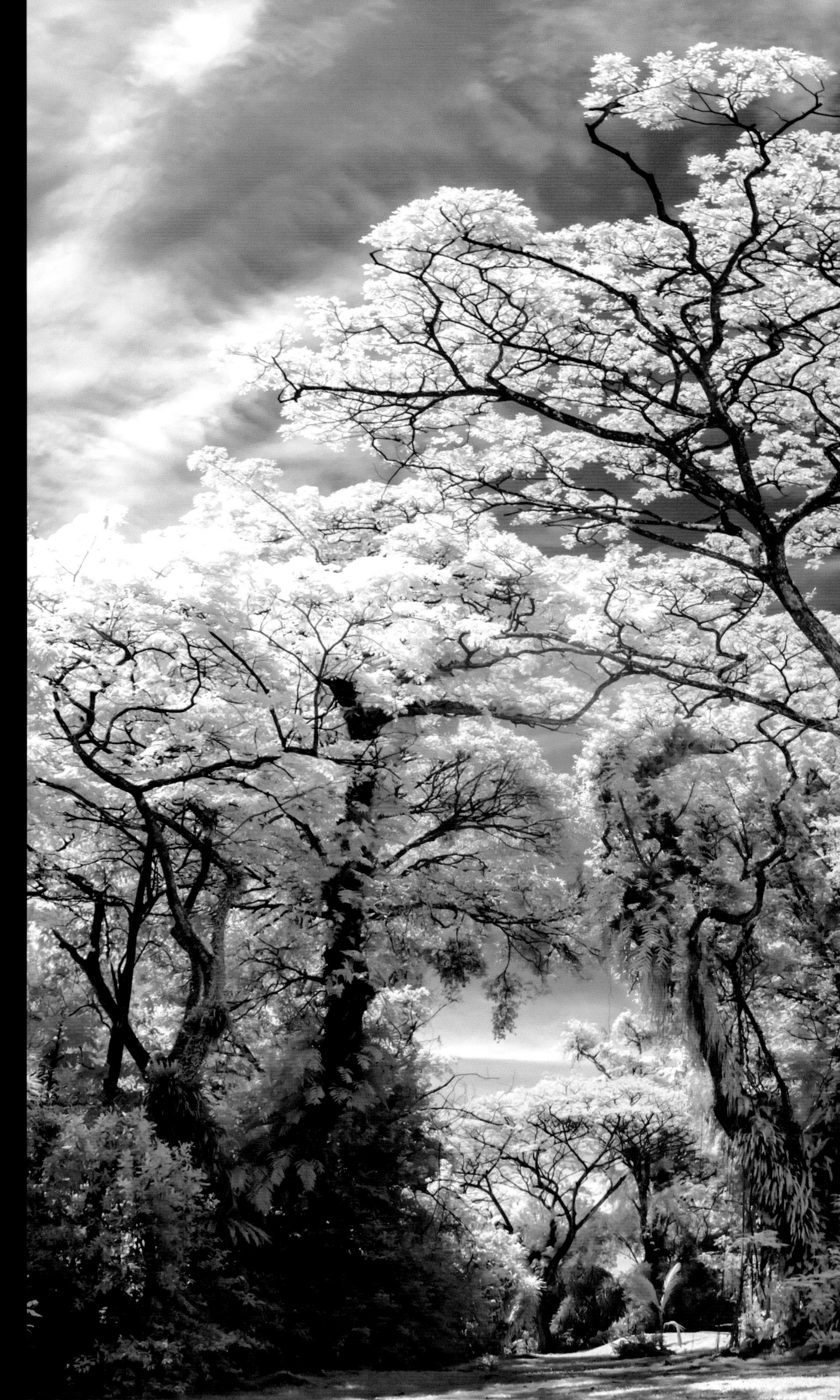

ea saman, Rain Tree

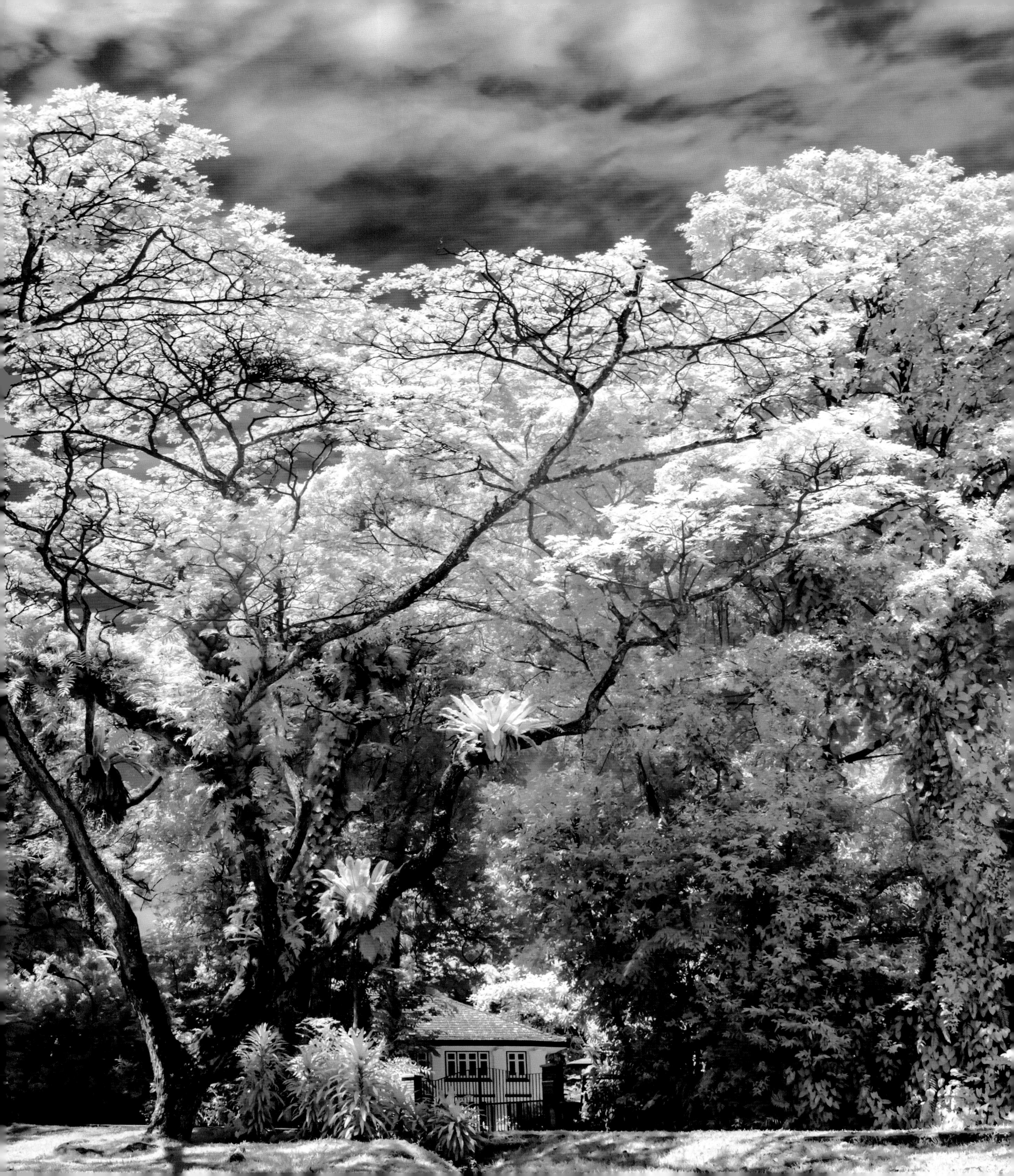

52 *Pterocarpus indicus*, Angsana

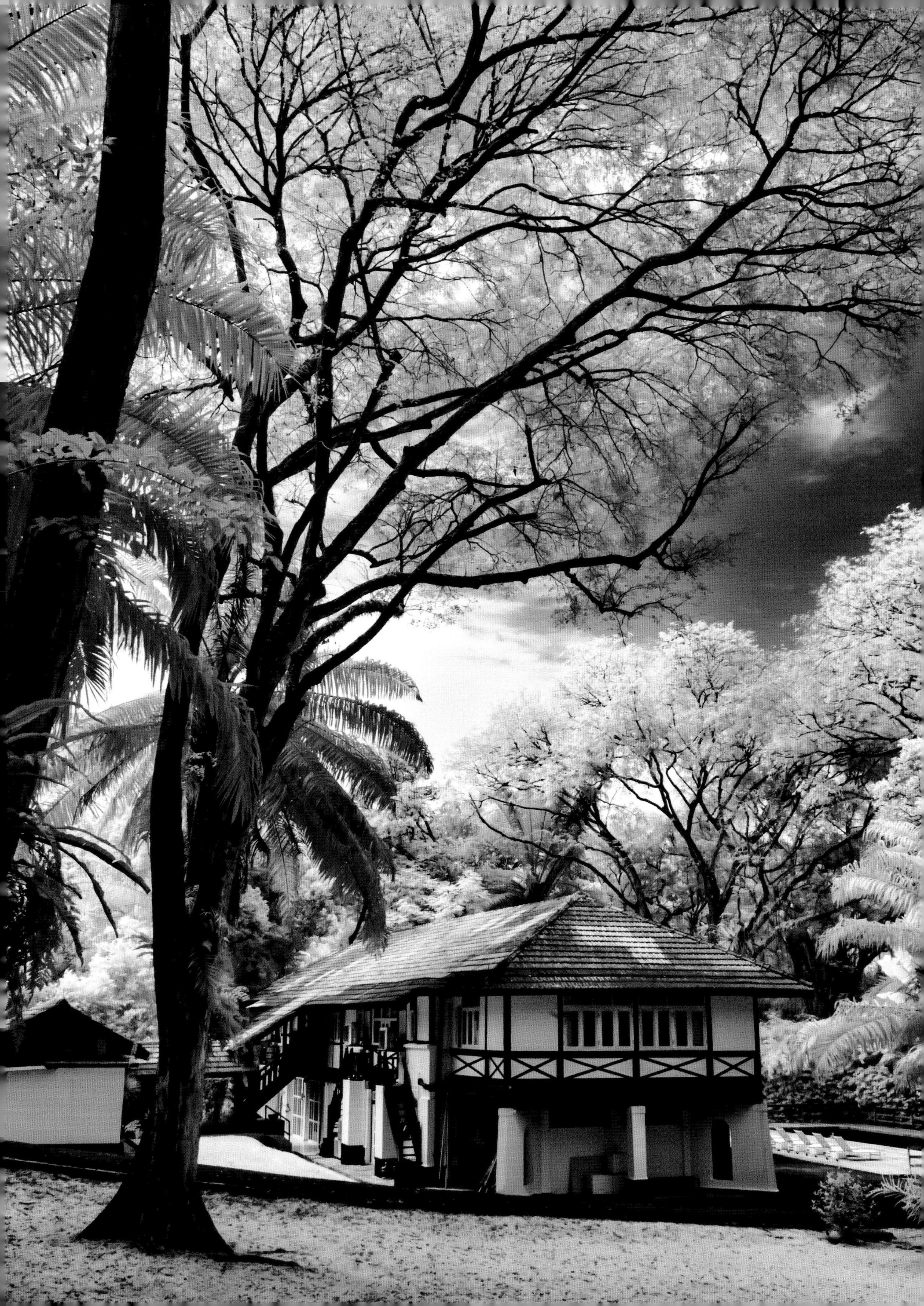

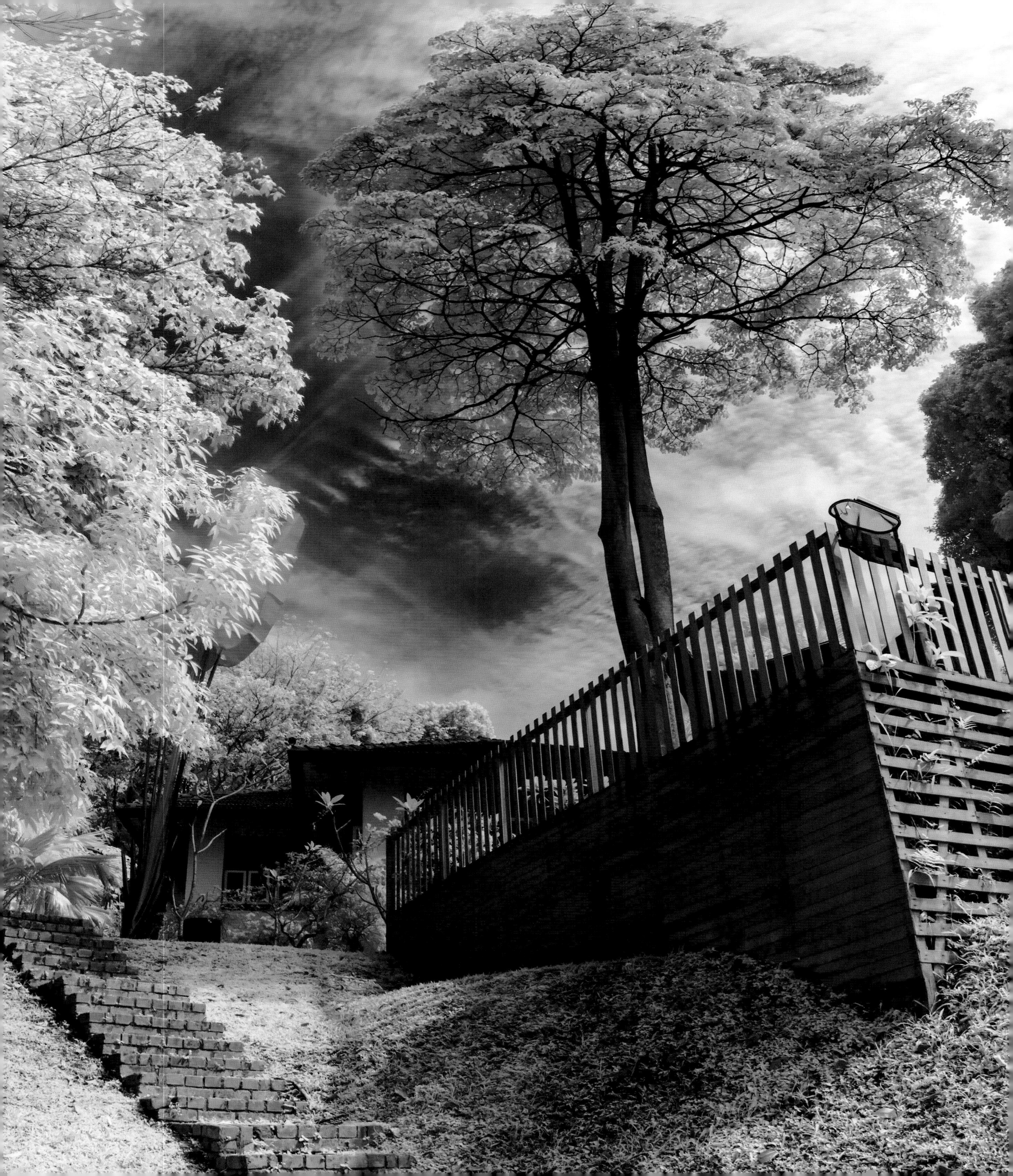

Alstonia angustiloba, Common Pulai

E J H Corner was the Assistant Director of the Singapore Botanic Gardens between 1929-1945. Together with the Director of the Botanic Gardens Richard E. Holttum, he was instrumental in ensuring the protected status of the Bukit Timah Nature Reserve in 1936.

During the Japanese occupation of Singapore he was responsible for the protection and preservation of the Botanic Gardens from looting and damage.

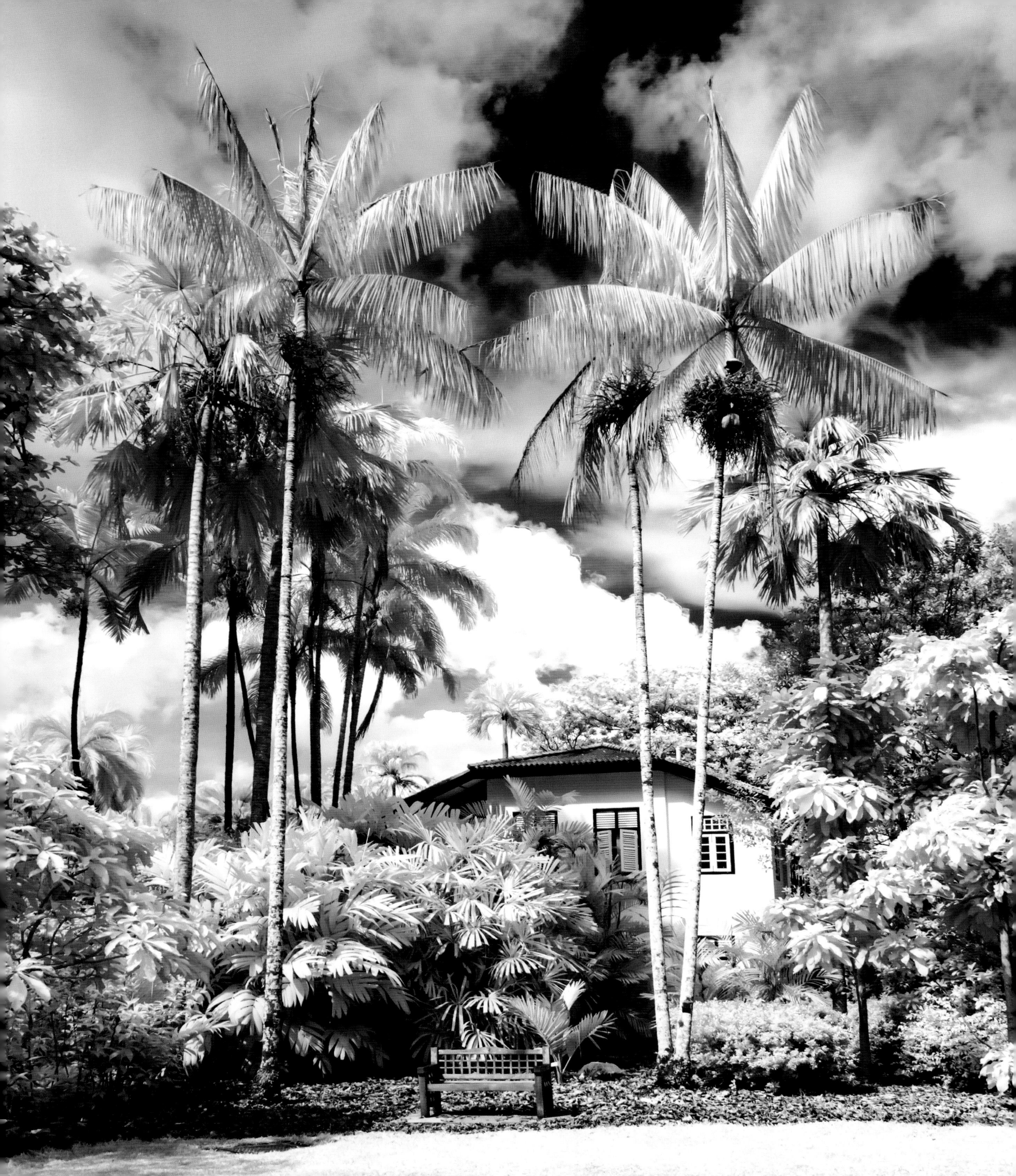

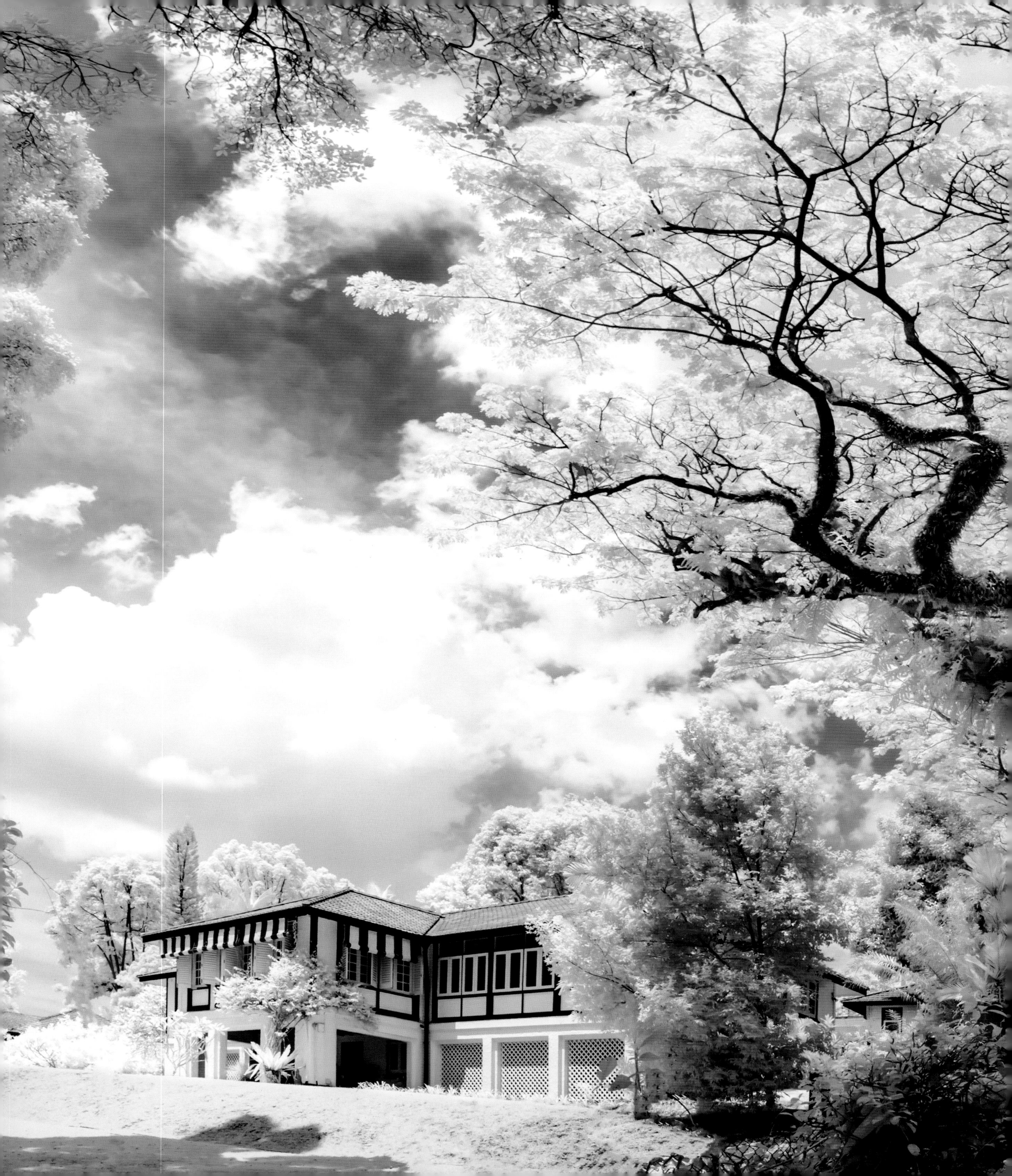

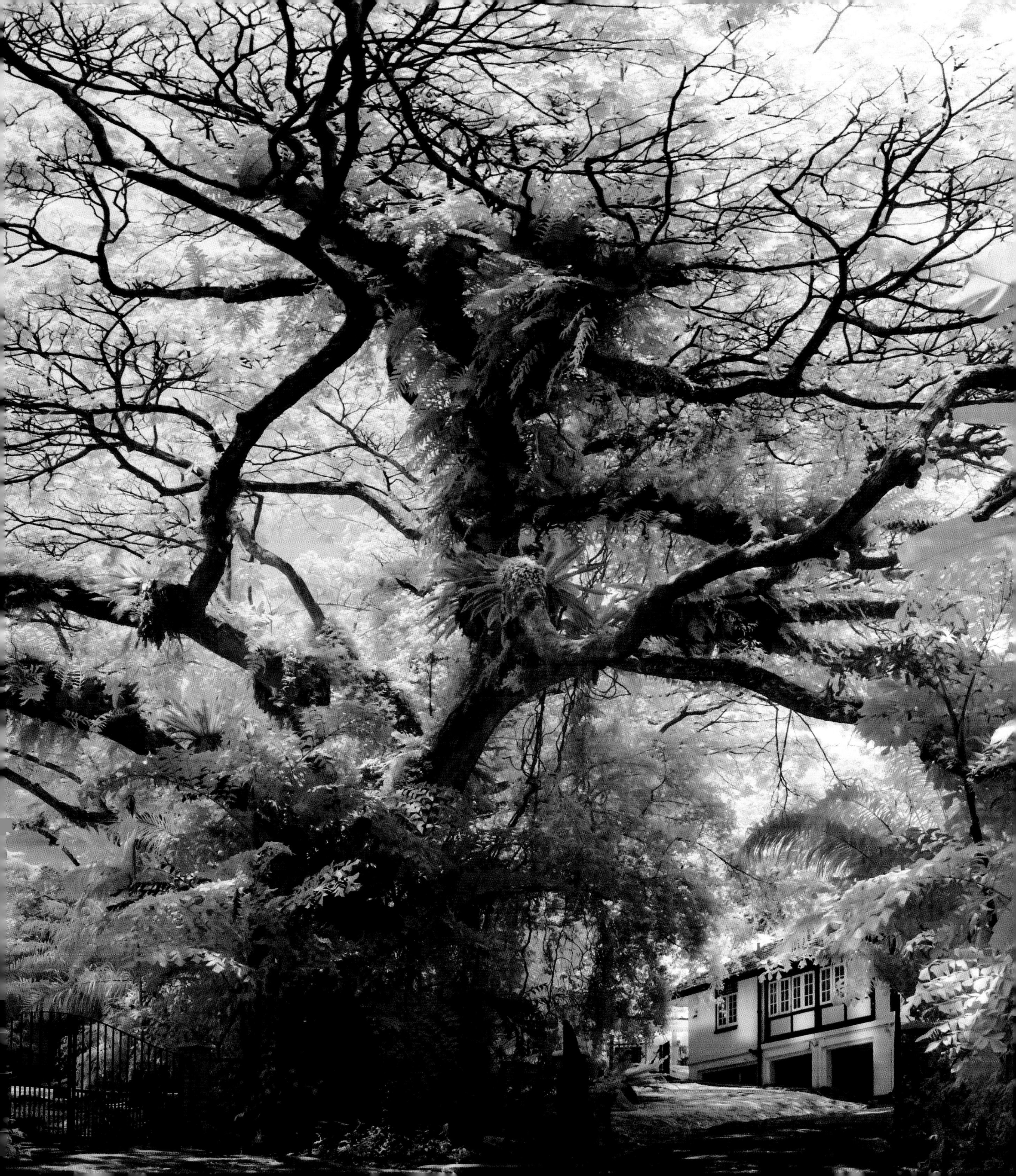

In Sembawang, the roads are mostly named after countries of the Commonwealth and former British colonies and territories.

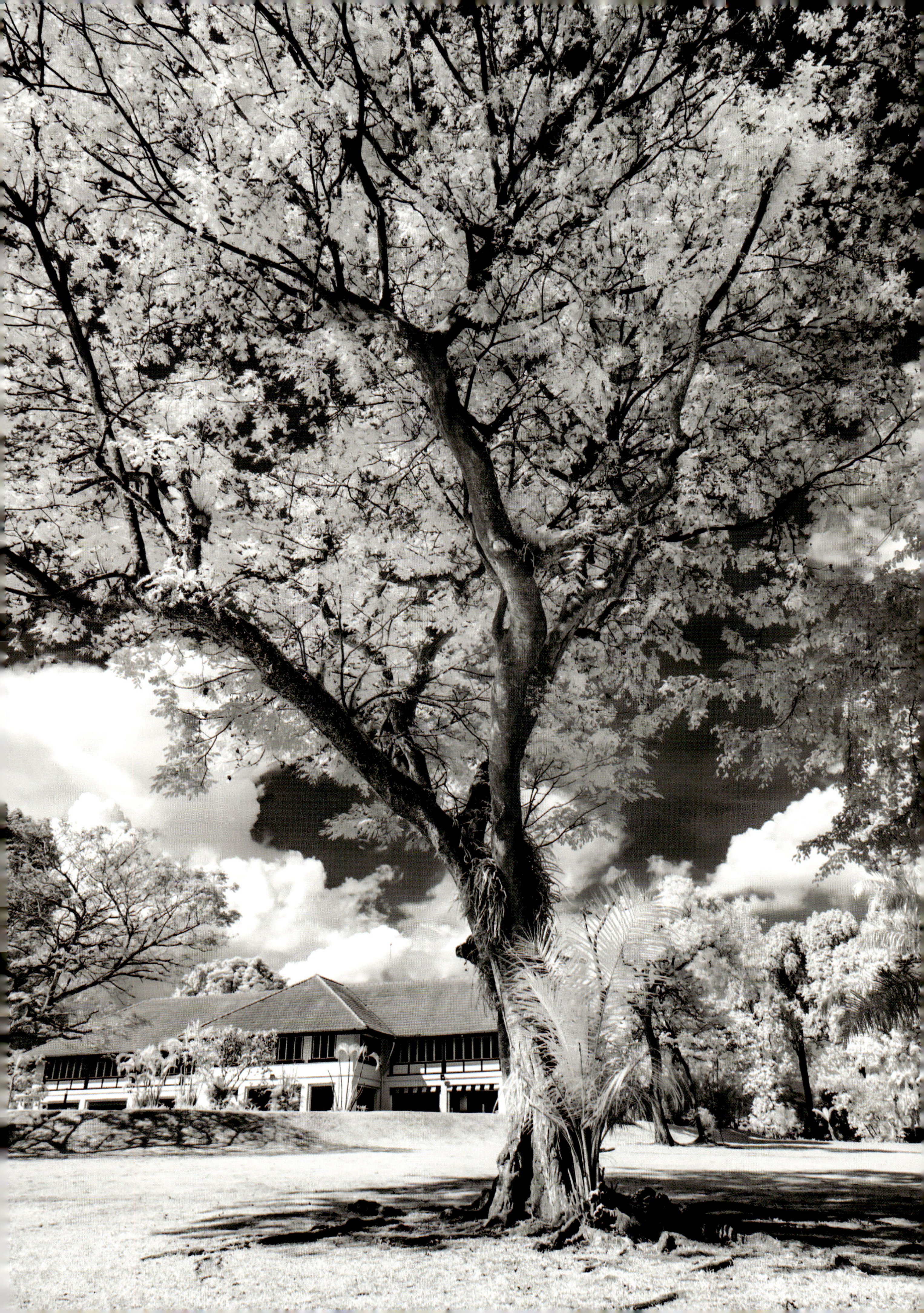

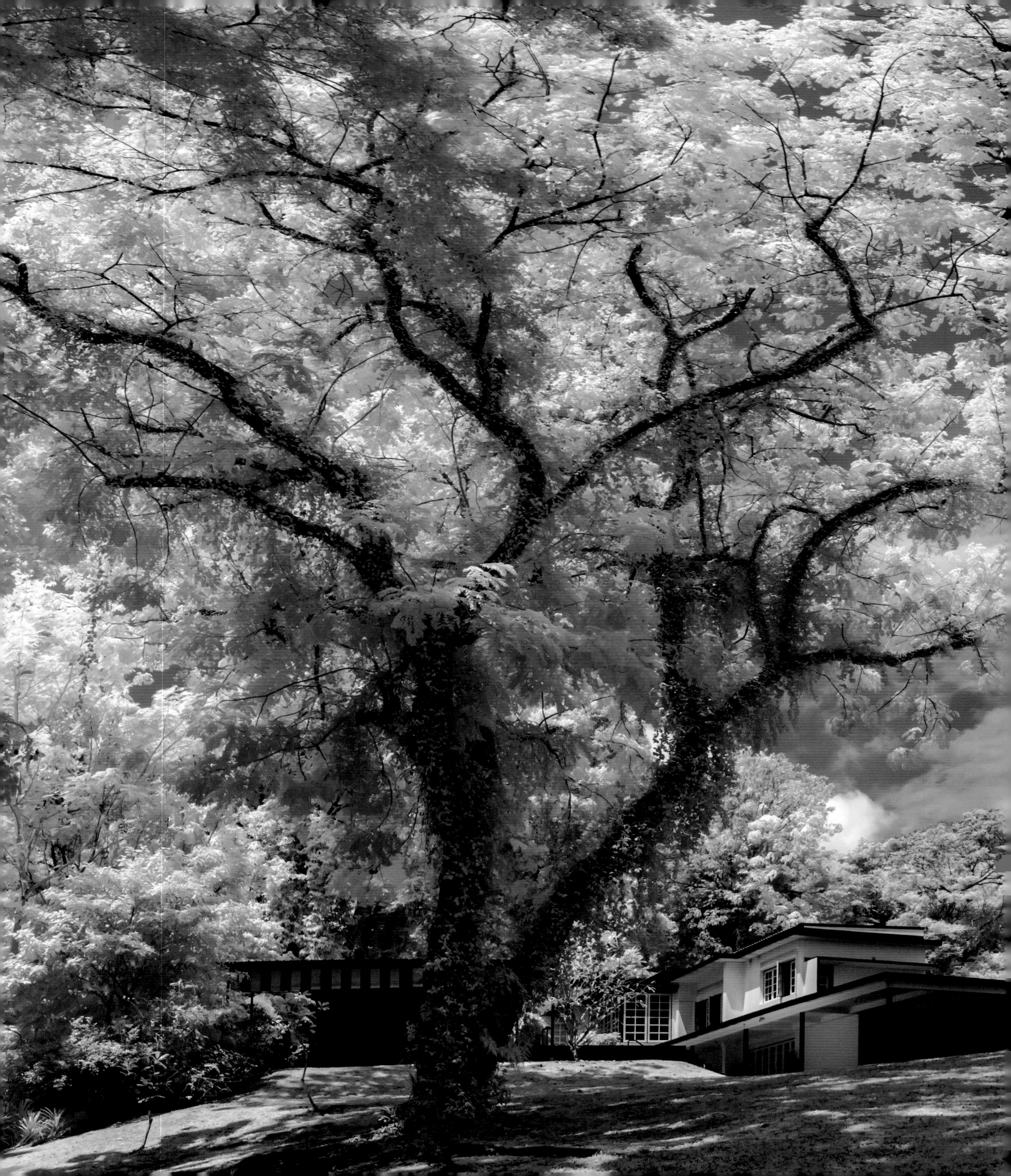

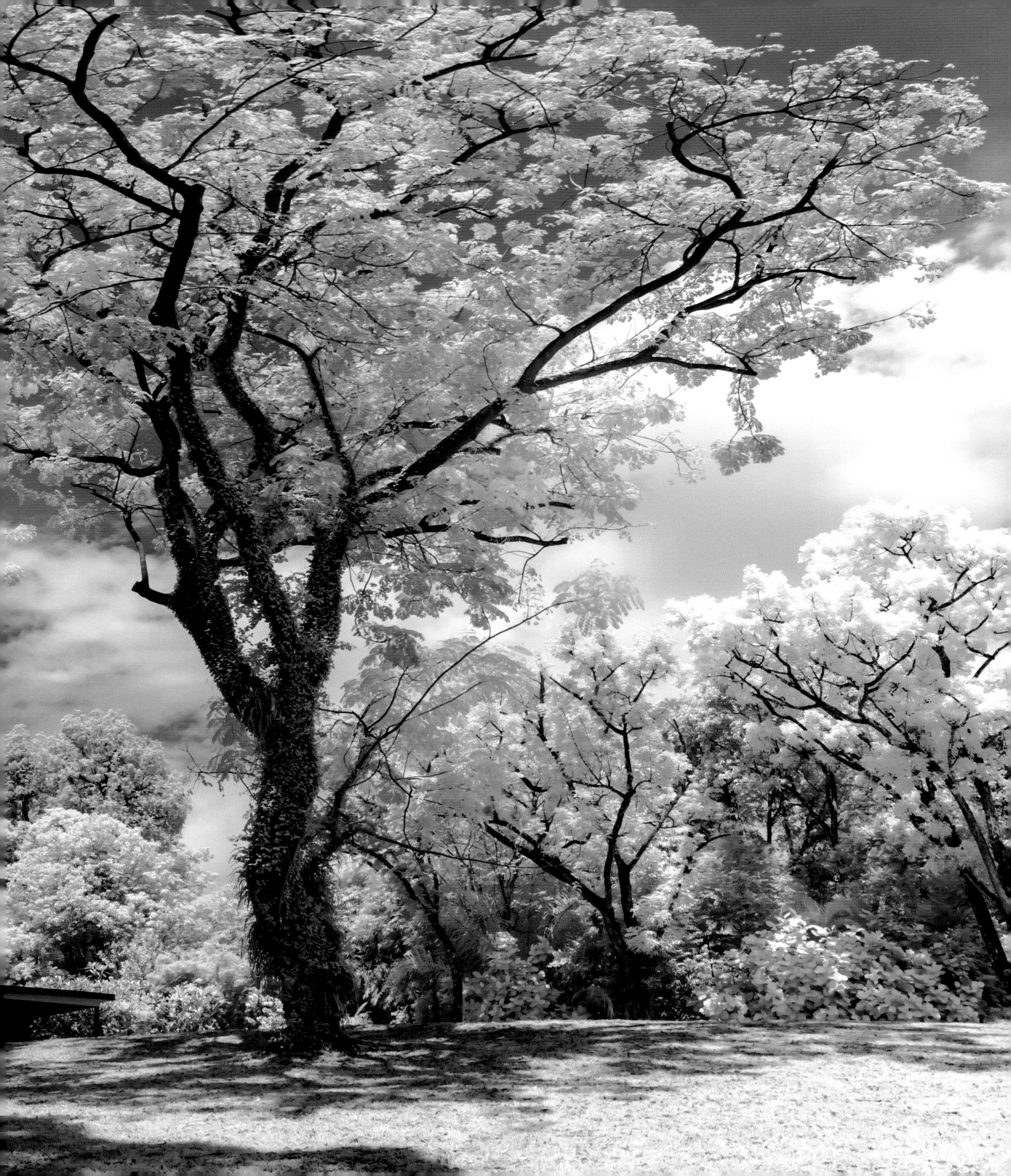

All the roads in the Wessex Estate are named after towns in England and start with 'W' such as Whitchurch Road or Woking Road.

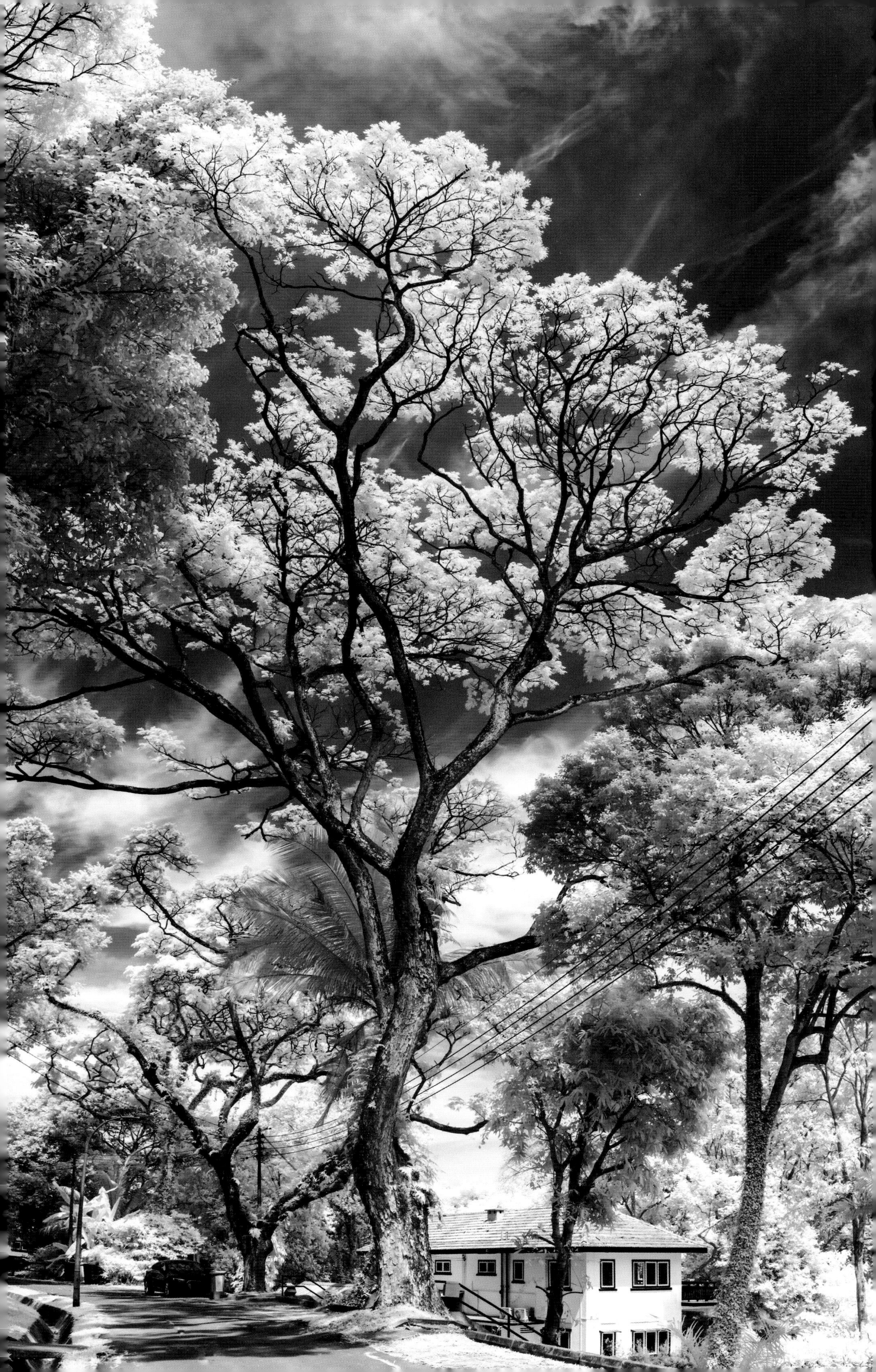

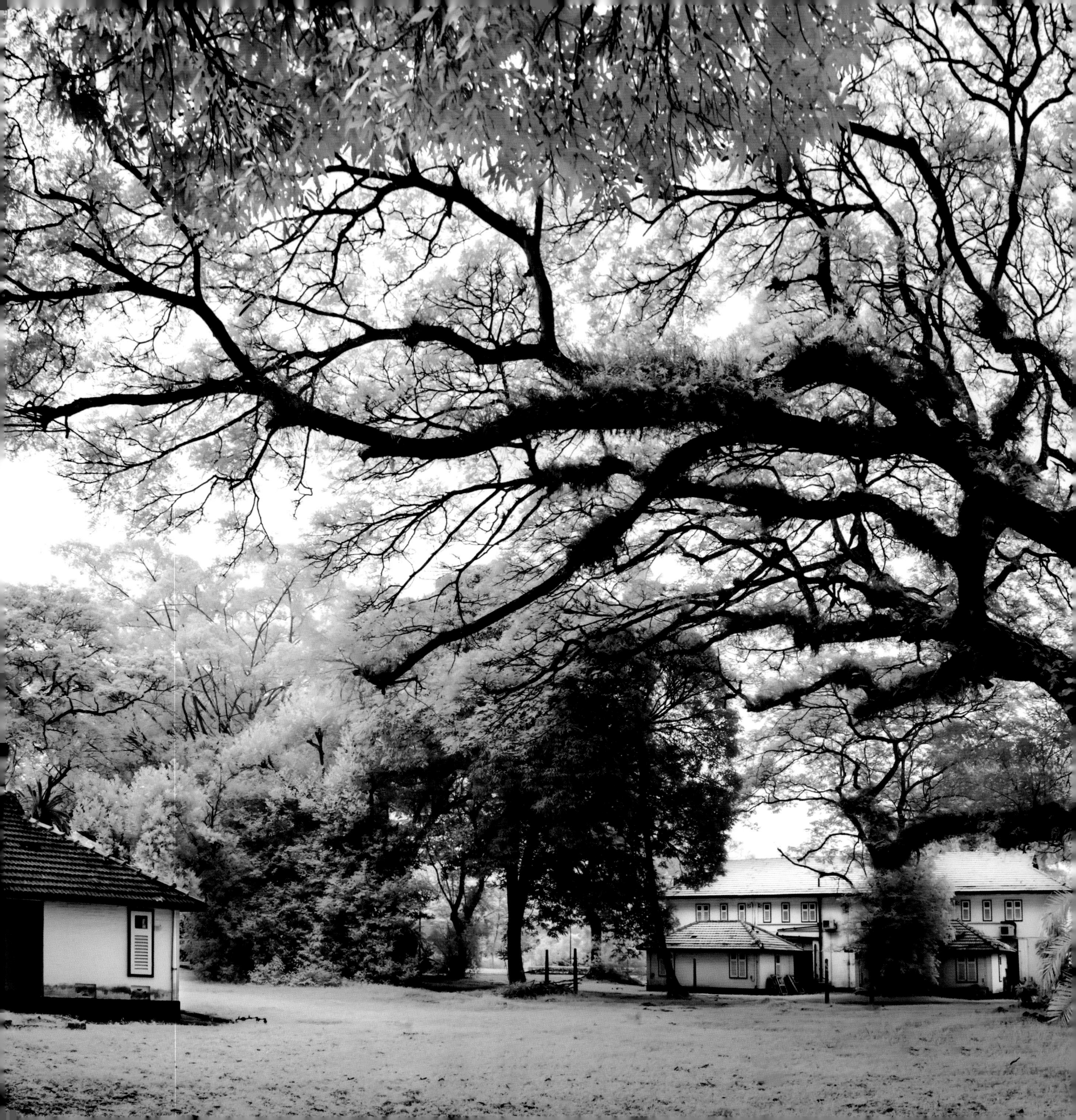

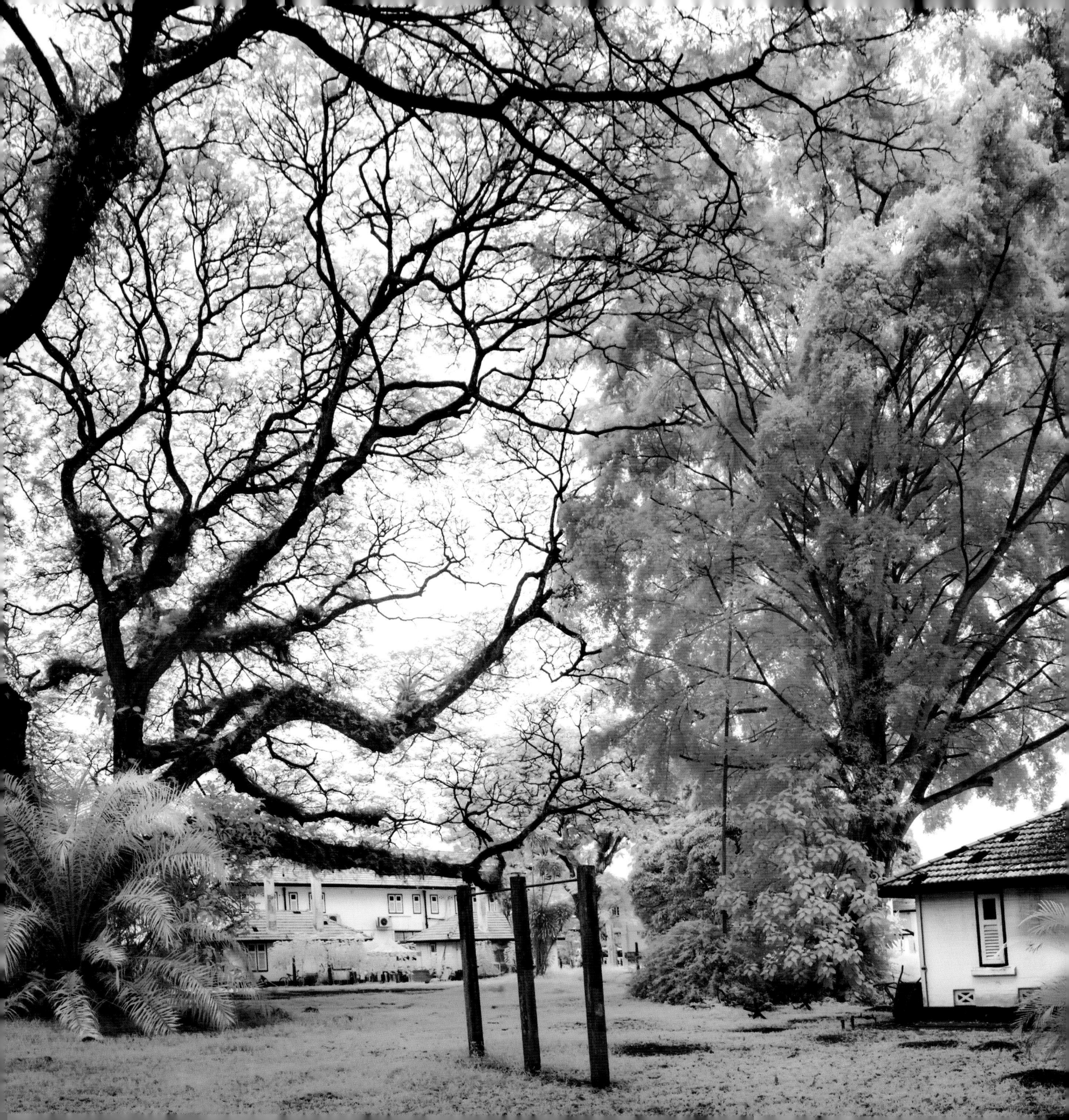

Henry Nicholas Ridley was appointed the first Director of the Singapore Botanic Garden in 1888. Besides rubber, he was also was a promoter of planting the Oil Palm in Singapore. So it is only natural that this photo should be taken in Ridley Park.

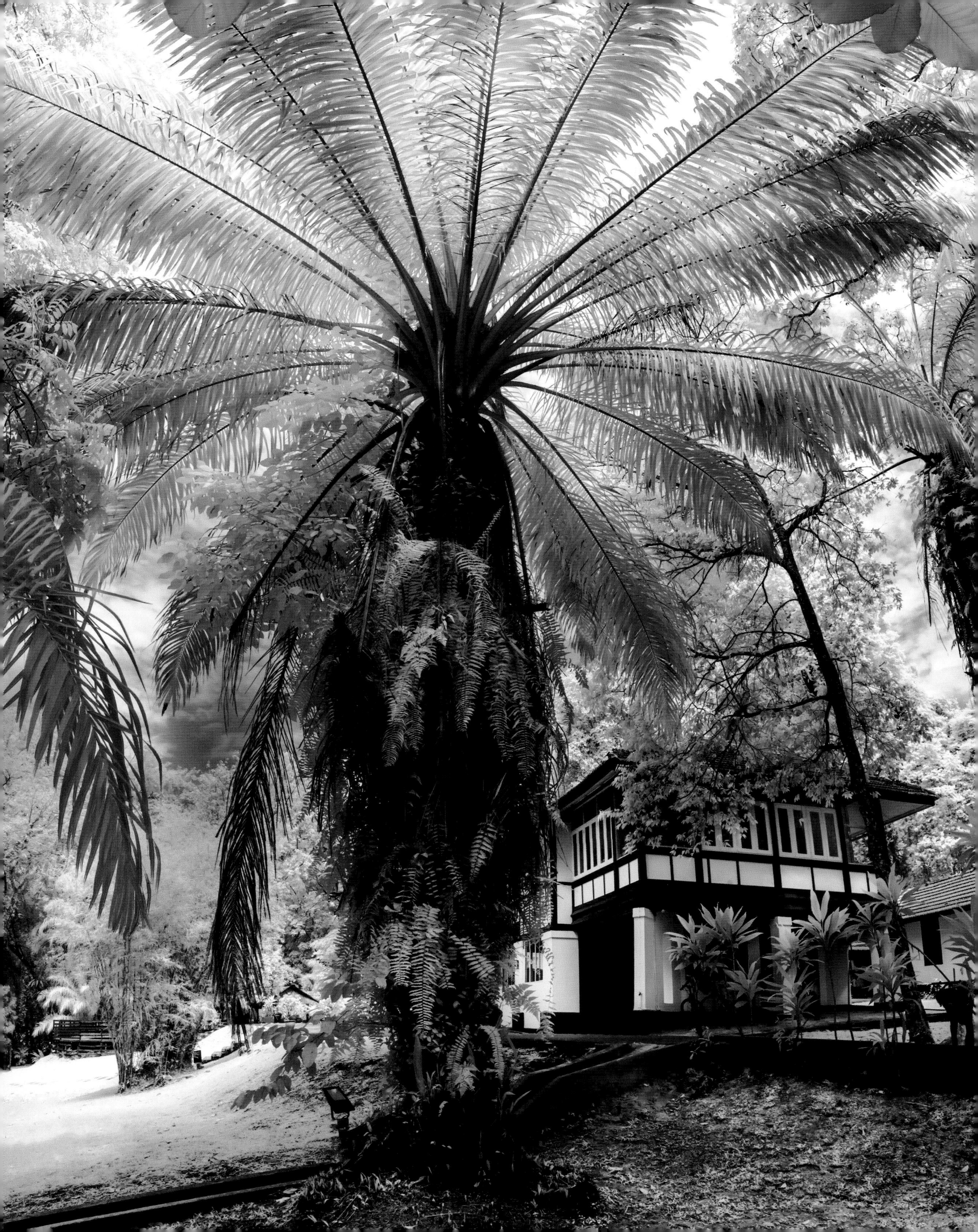

You can often tell the age of a tree by how many epiphytes are growing on it. As the tree matures the epiphyte grows with it.

Including the Bird's Nest Fern and the Davallia Fern, this Rain Tree has at least two different types of epiphytes growing on it.

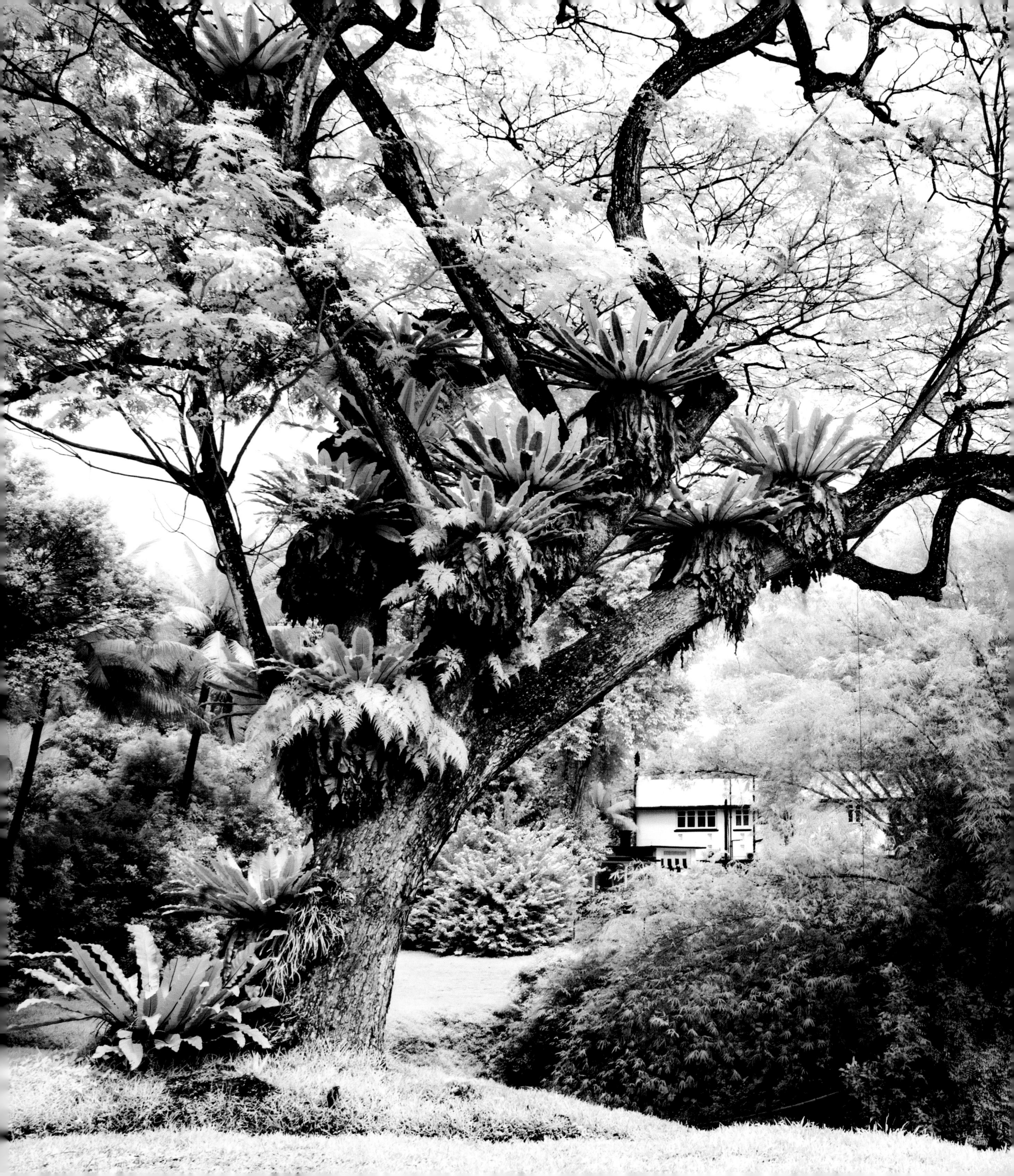

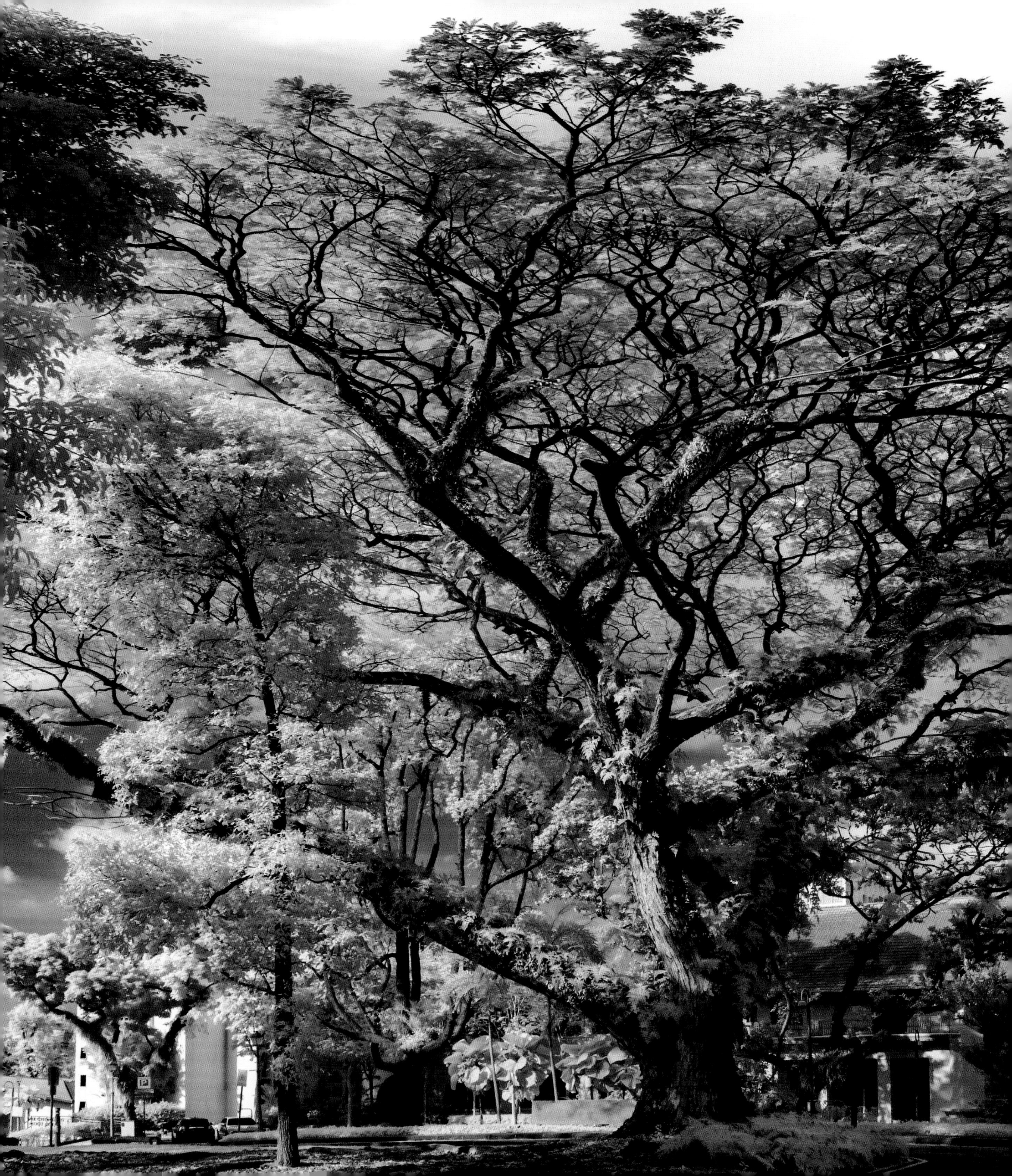

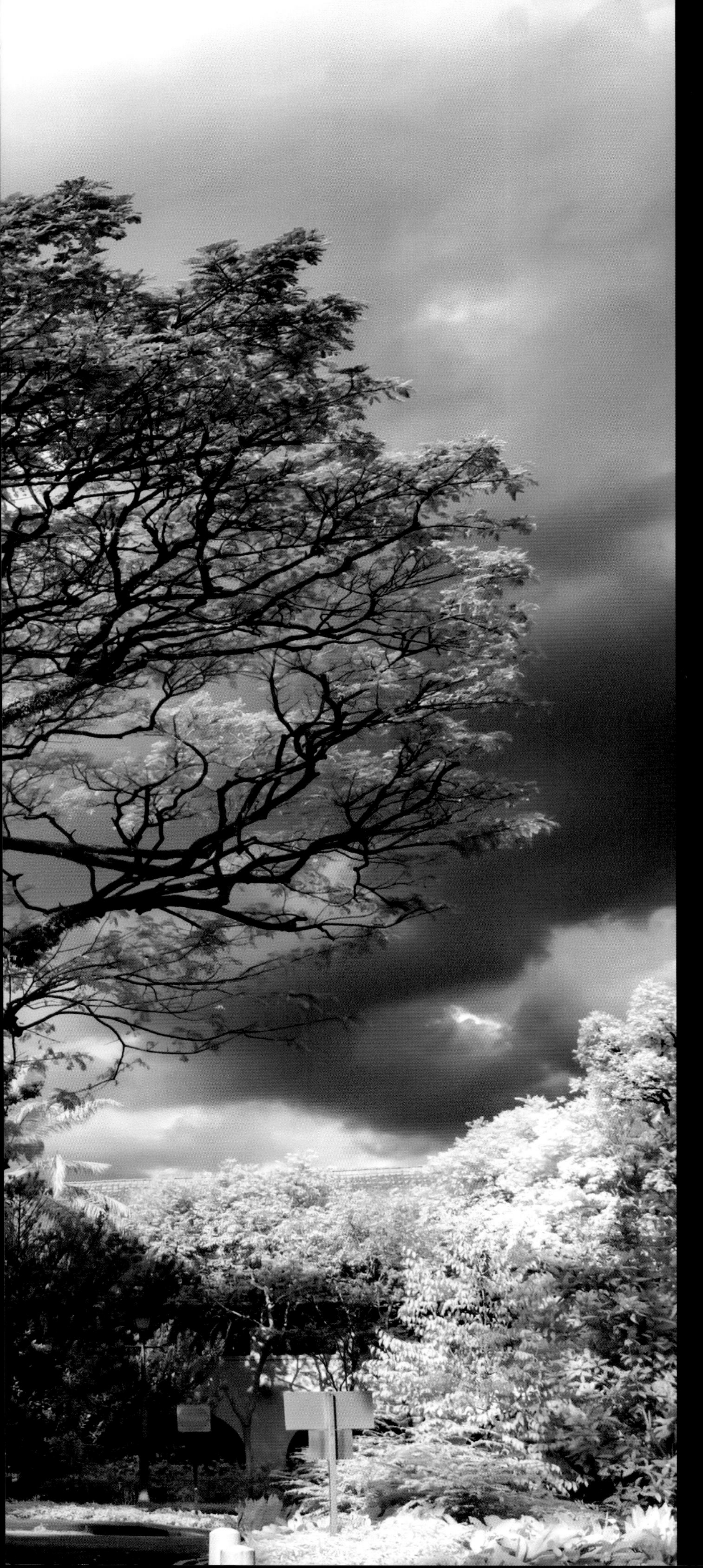

Samanea saman, Rain Tree

"Set on the highest point on the hill the house has the largest gardens and most impressive view."

The Adam Park Project, Metal Detector Survey Report No. 11

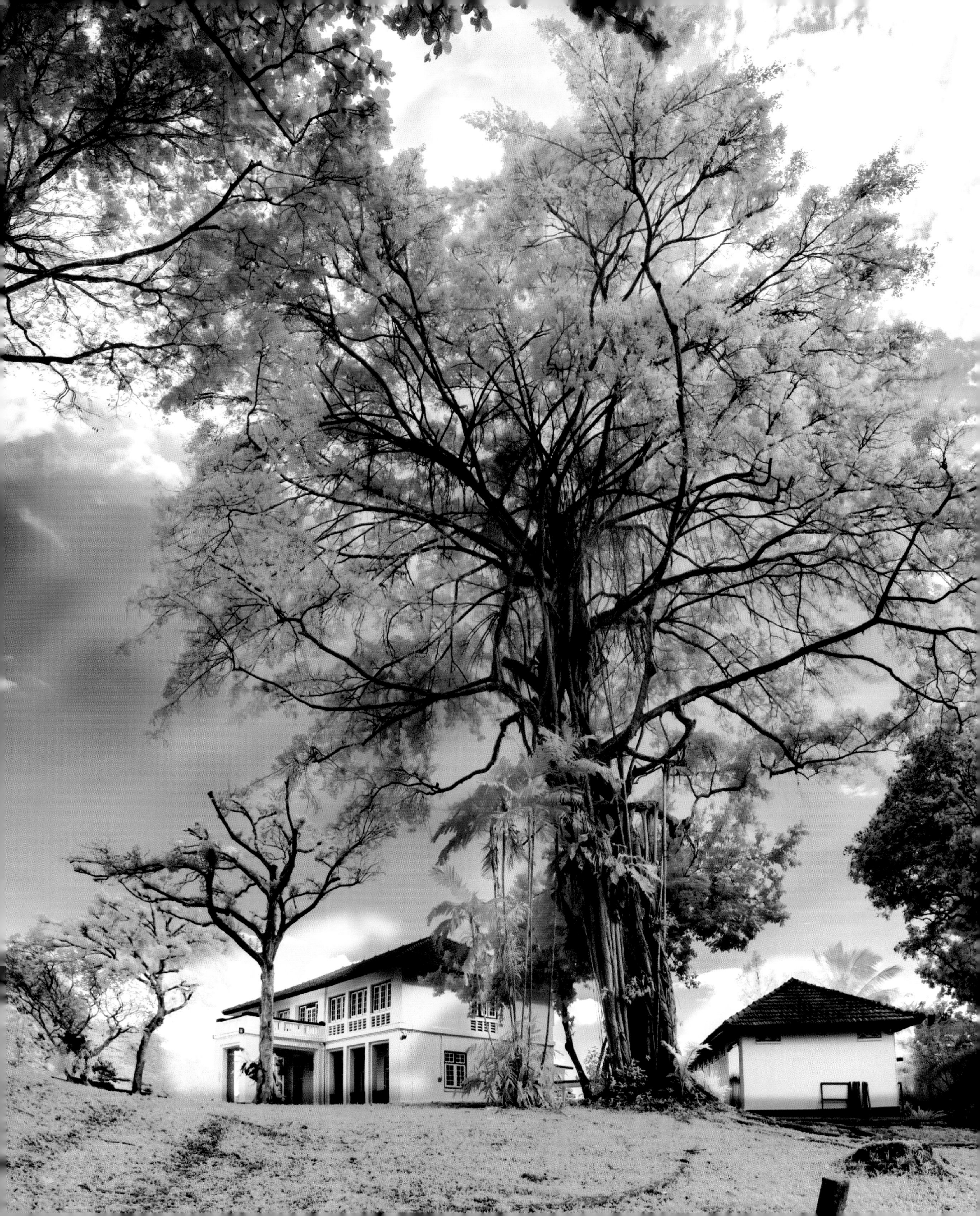

Wee Kay Siang, for whom Kay Siang Road is named, died in Singapore on 31 July 1925. He was a founder of a Chinese bank in Singapore and a director of the old Singapore Opium Farmers.

Before being renamed Kay Siang Road, this black and white enclave was part of the Ridley Park estate.

Source: *Straits Budget*, 7 August 1925

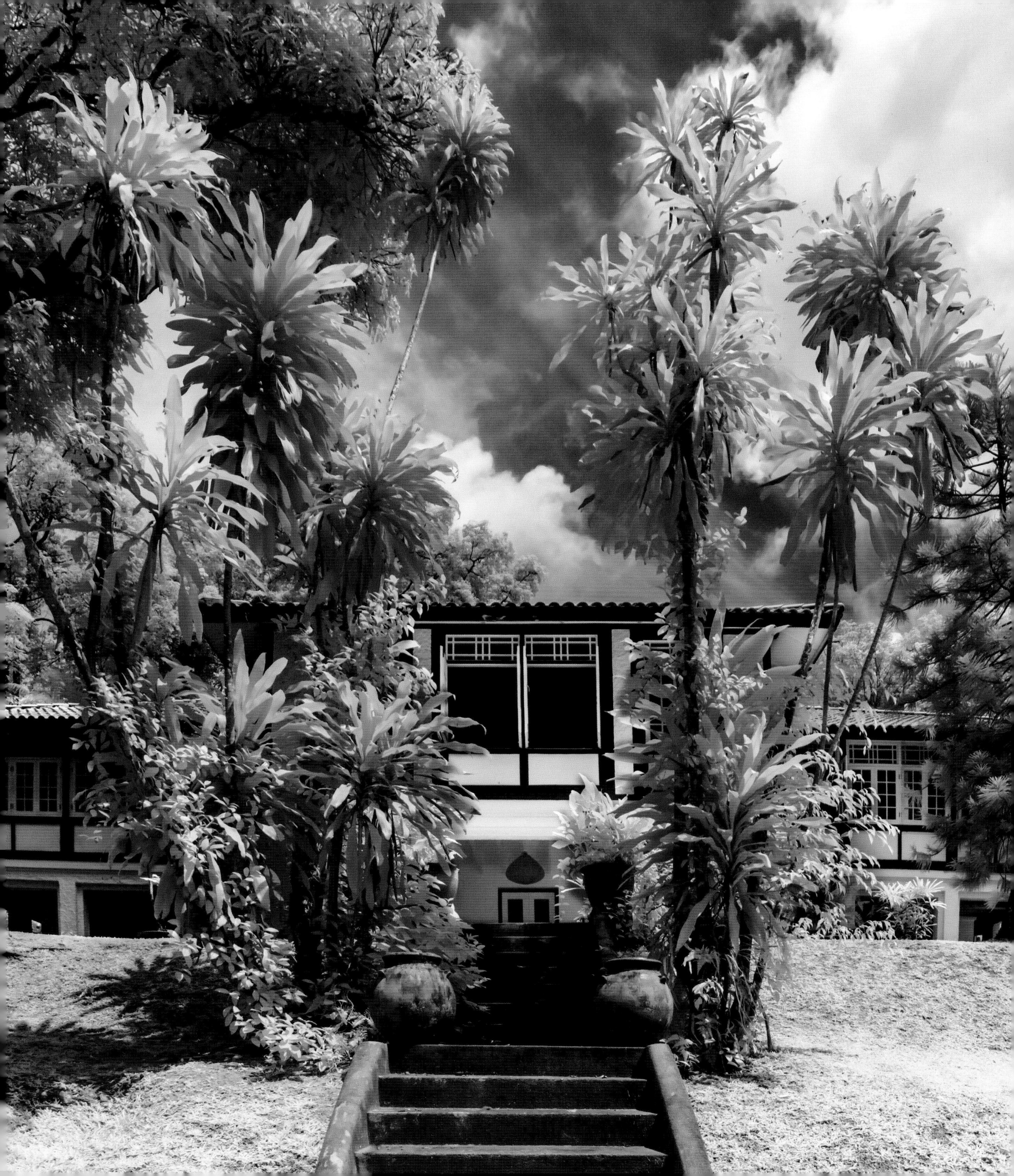

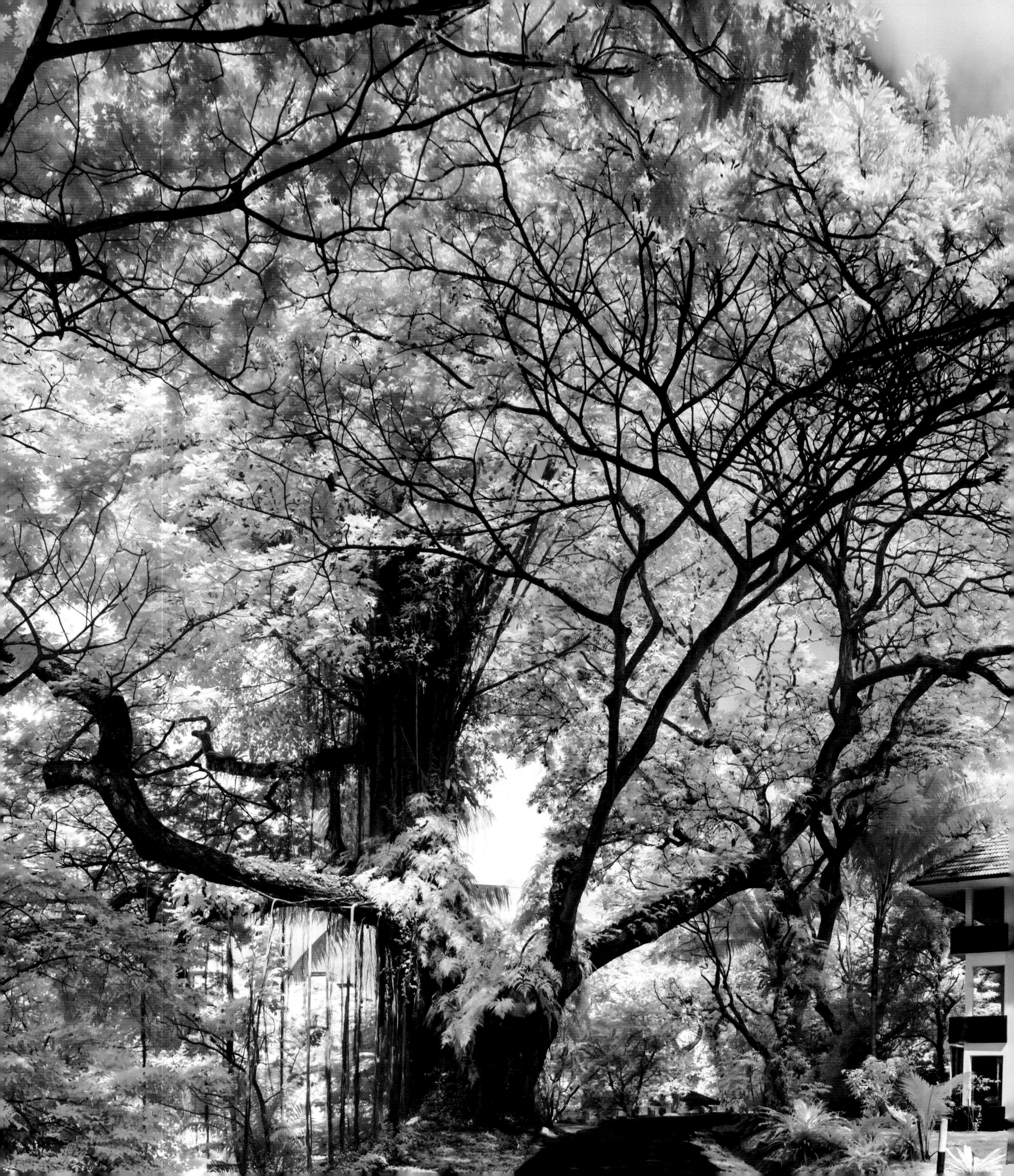

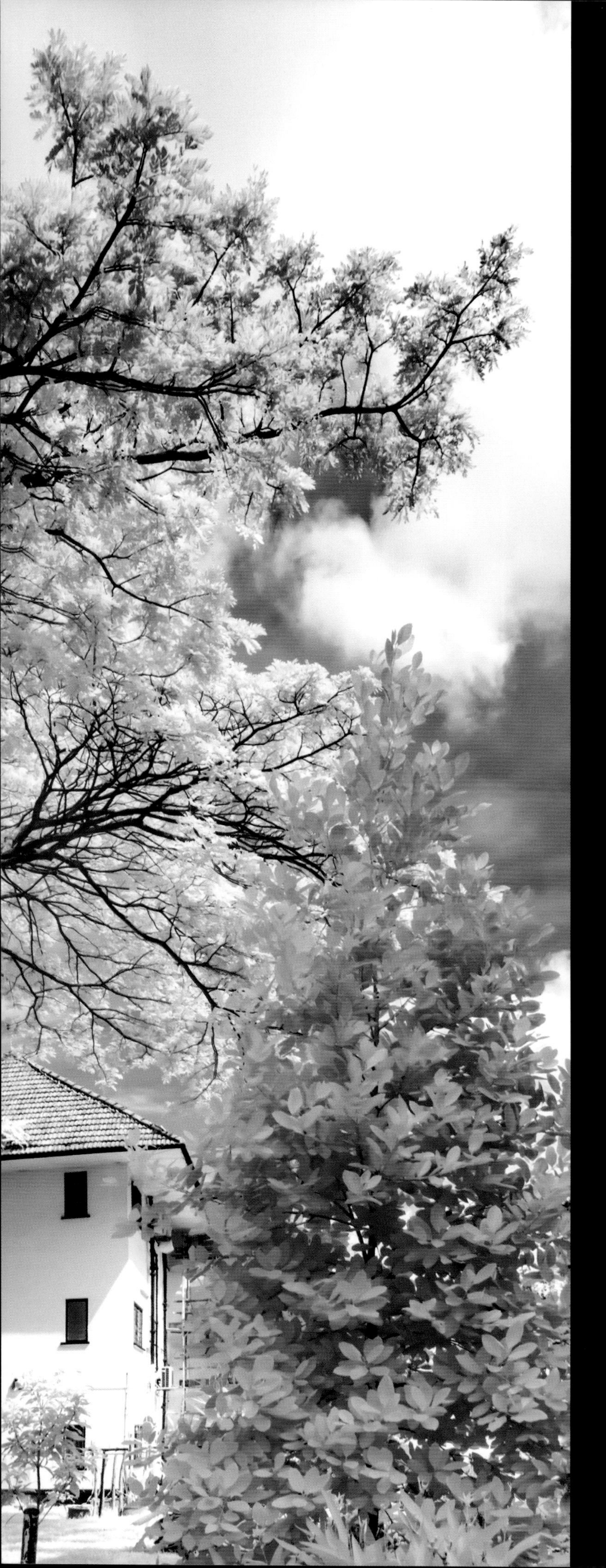

Samanea saman, Rain

The Singapore Turf Club was built on 244 acres of land that was purchased from the Bukit Timah Rubber Estate in 1927. The iconic North Grandstand towers over the bungalows and was originally built for the purpose of housing the senior managers of the club.

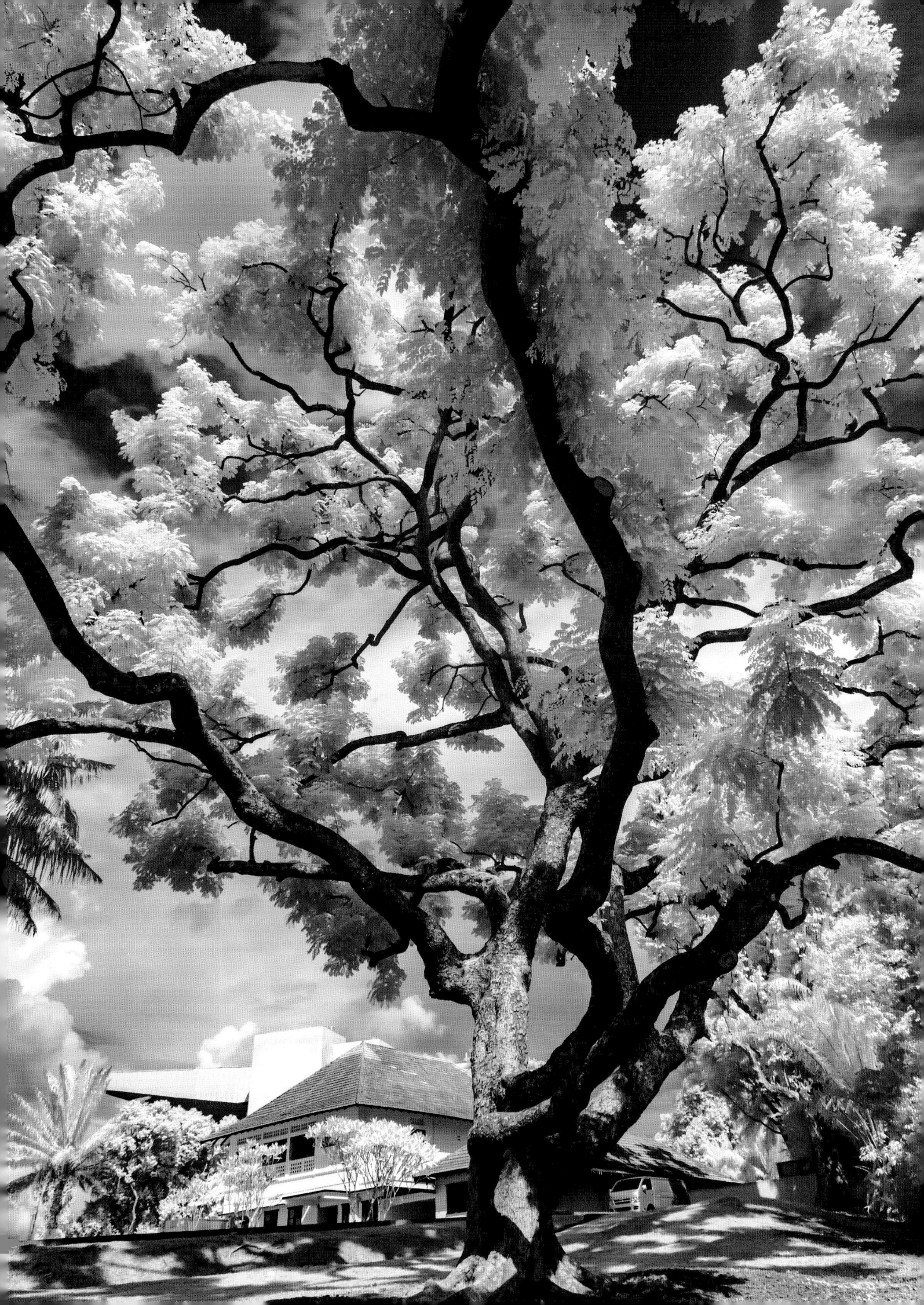

Although the Rain Tree is synonymous with Singapore, it is actually not native to Singapore and had been imported into Singapore in and around 1876.

The Rain Tree is native to Central America but can now be found throughout Southeast Asia.

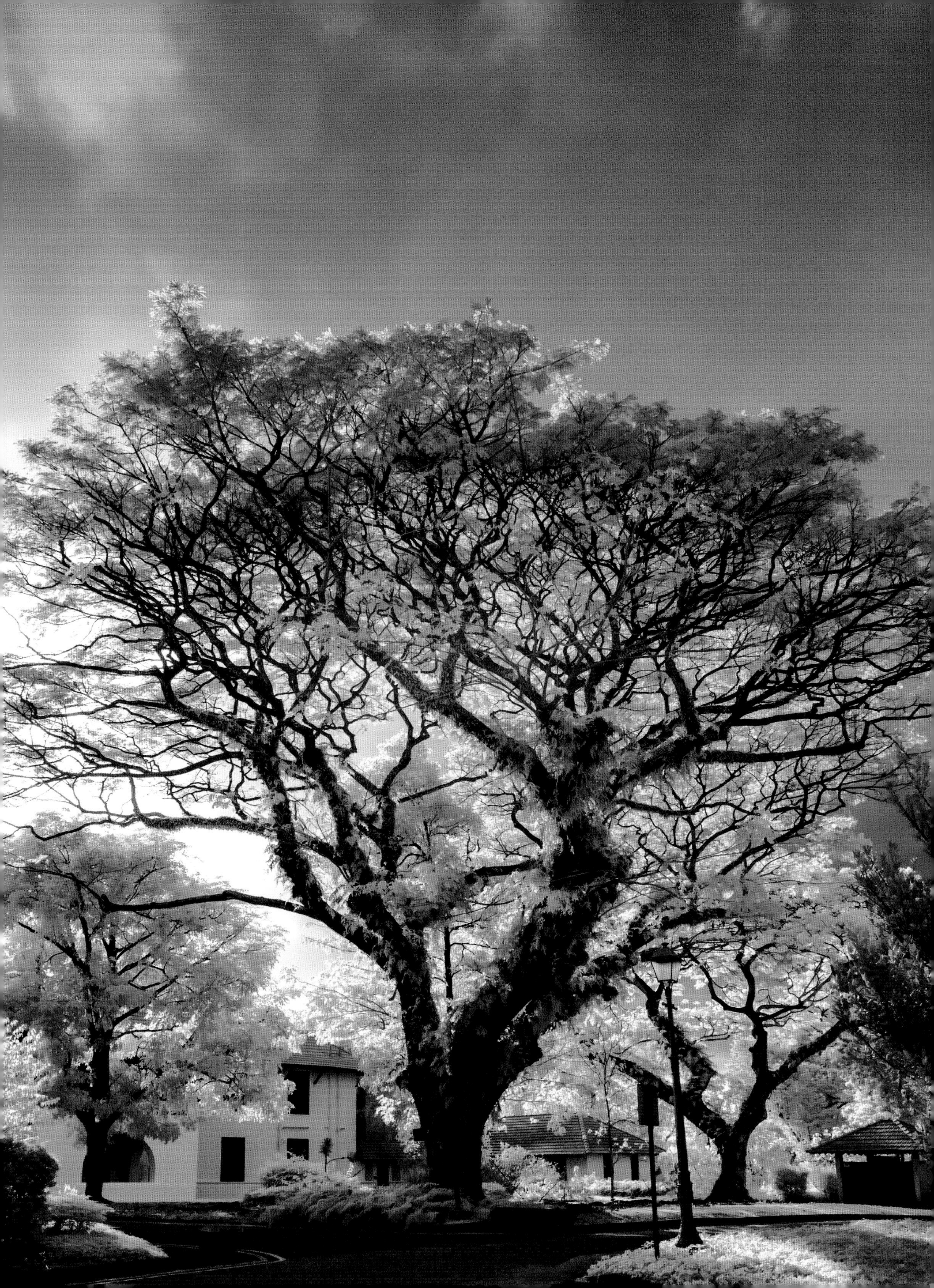

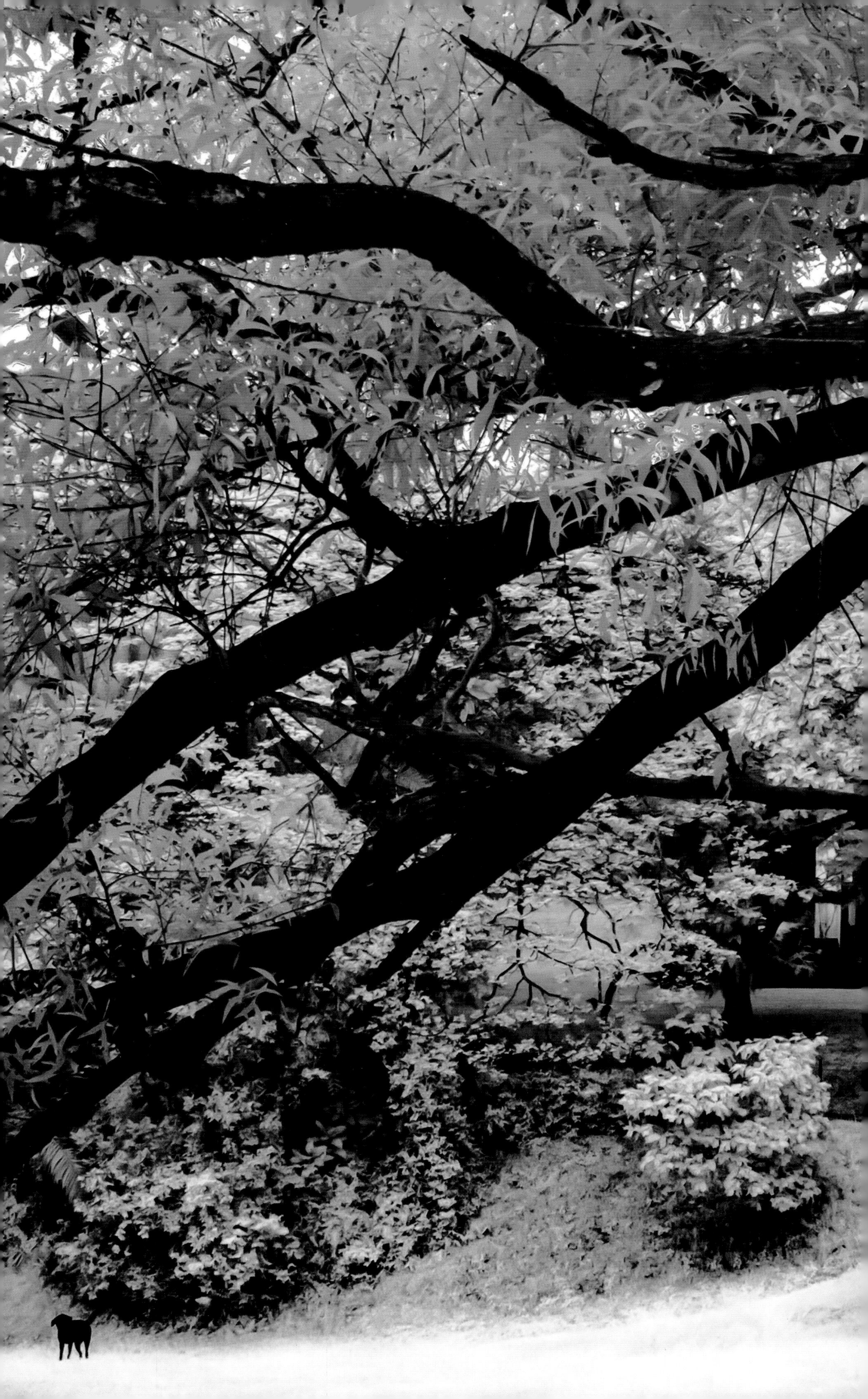

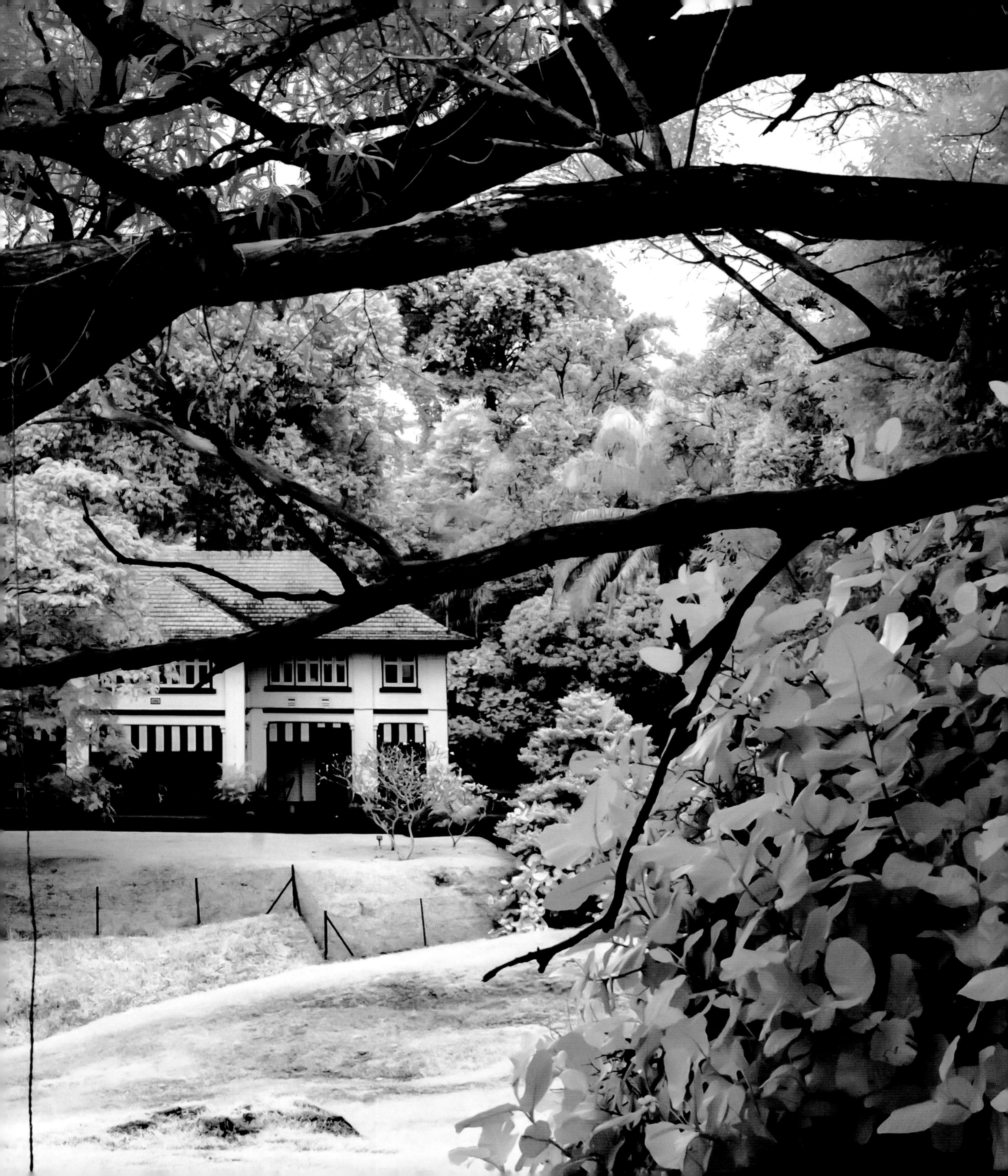

For this project, when photographing in the grounds of the black and white house I was visiting, I'd usually ask the tenants whether they had snakes in their garden - so that I could take precautions.

The usual answer was a mention of a cobra or python that resided somewhere on the grounds. However, when visiting this house, I was told to keep an eye out for the resident monitor lizard. I didn't spot it during the shoot; however, when I was editing this photograph, sure enough, there it was - halfway up the Alstonia.

 Alstonia angustiloba, Common Pulai

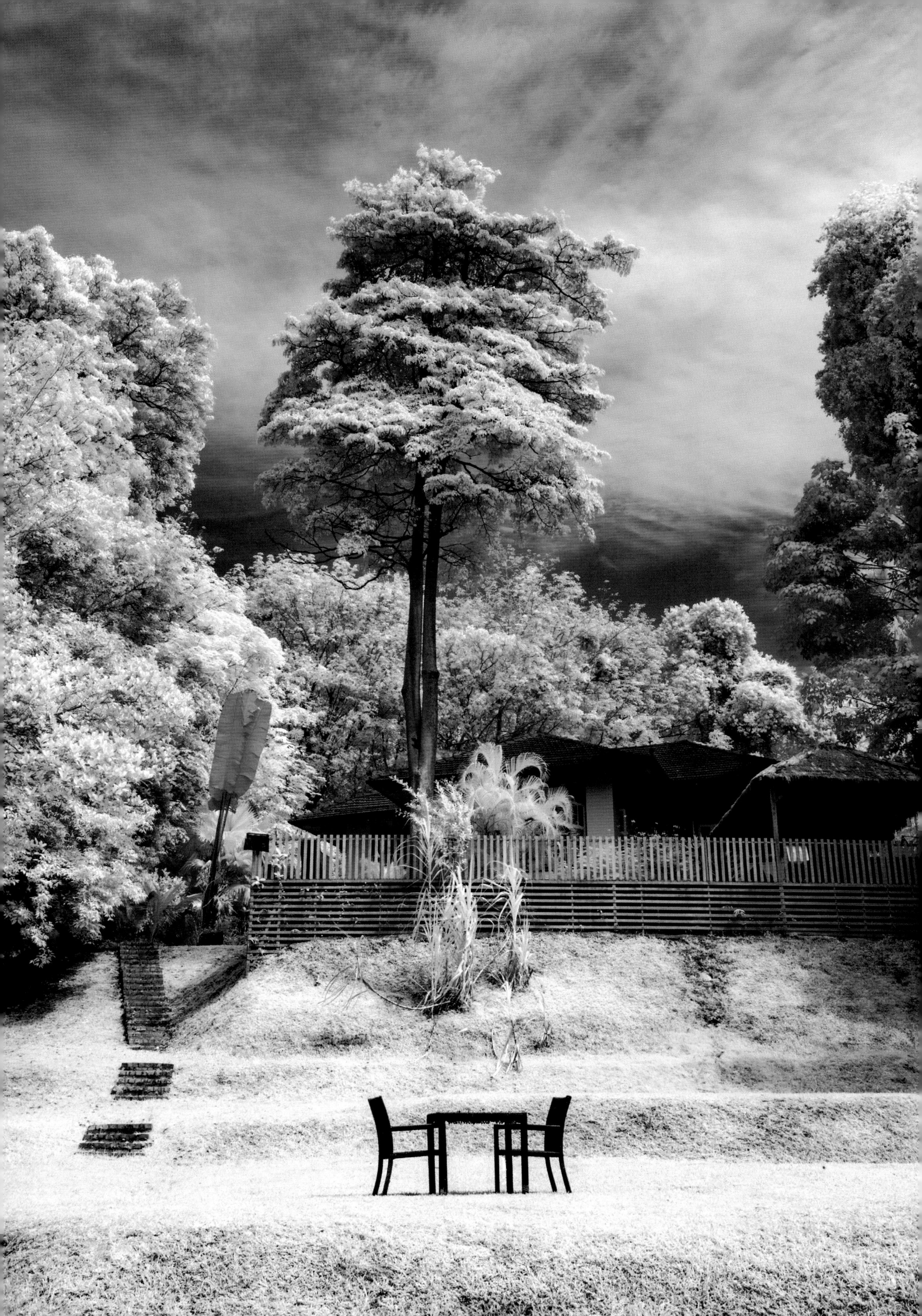

The Yellow Flame tree is native to Singapore. It is a critically endangered species in Singapore although abundant in South East Asia. When the tree flowers, it produces thin, flat, copper-colored pods which is why it's is also known as the Copperpod Tree.

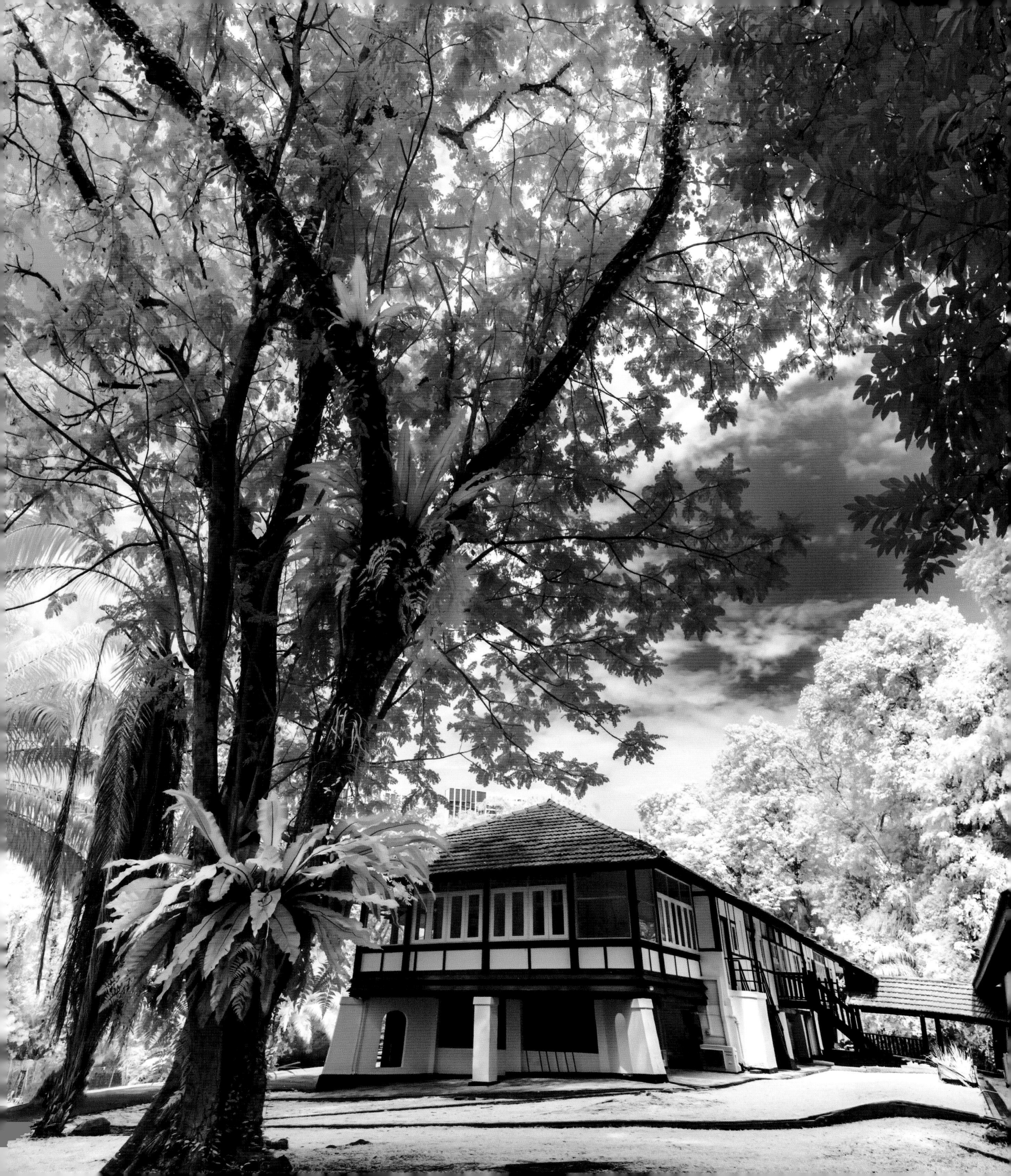

"The sun rose to the mid sky and doves cooed in the shade. Withered leaves danced and whirled in the hot air of noon. The shepherd boy drowsed and dreamed in the shadow of the banyan tree, and I laid myself down by the water and stretched my tired limbs on the grass."

Rabindranath Tagore, Gitanjali: Song Offerings

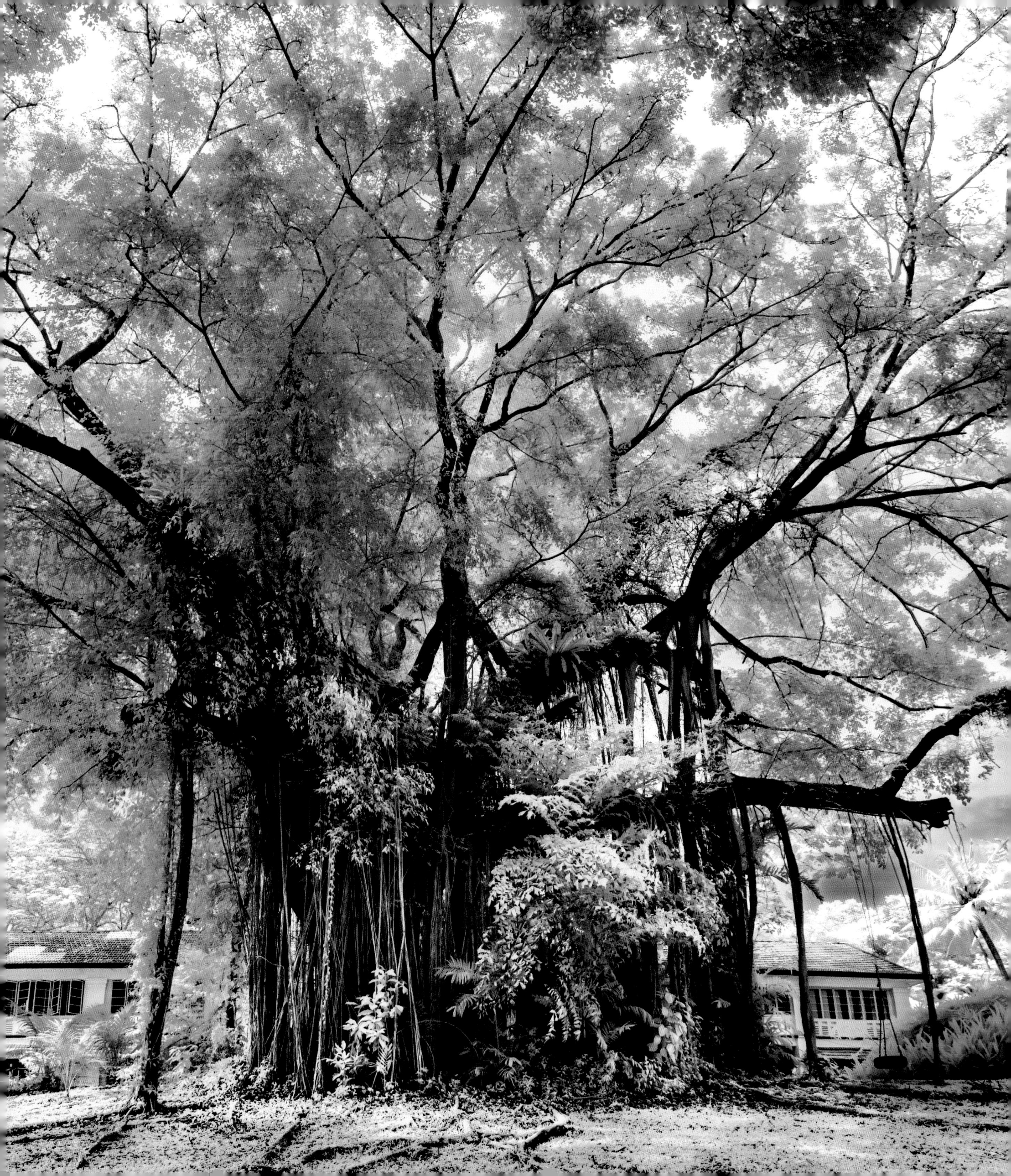

Many Angsana trees were planted in Singapore during the 1967 Garden City programme launched by former Prime Minister Lee Kwan Yew, with the idea of creating tree-lined boulevards across Singapore.

According to an article written in 1972, of the 110 road side species of trees in Singapore, only 15 were indigenous to Singapore.

Betty L. Khoo, The Botanic Garden - where native plants grow undisturbed; *New Nation*, 21 July 1972

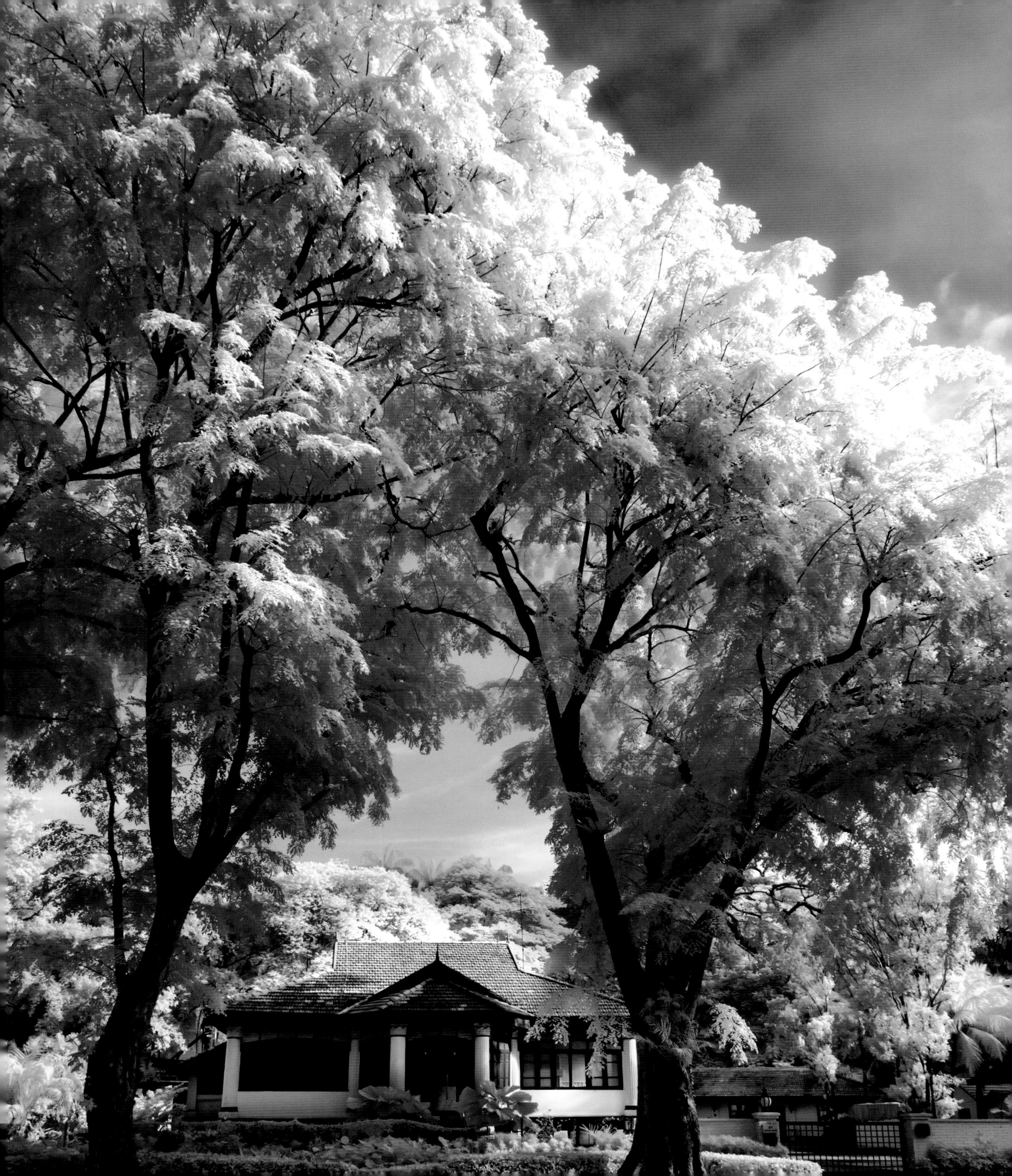

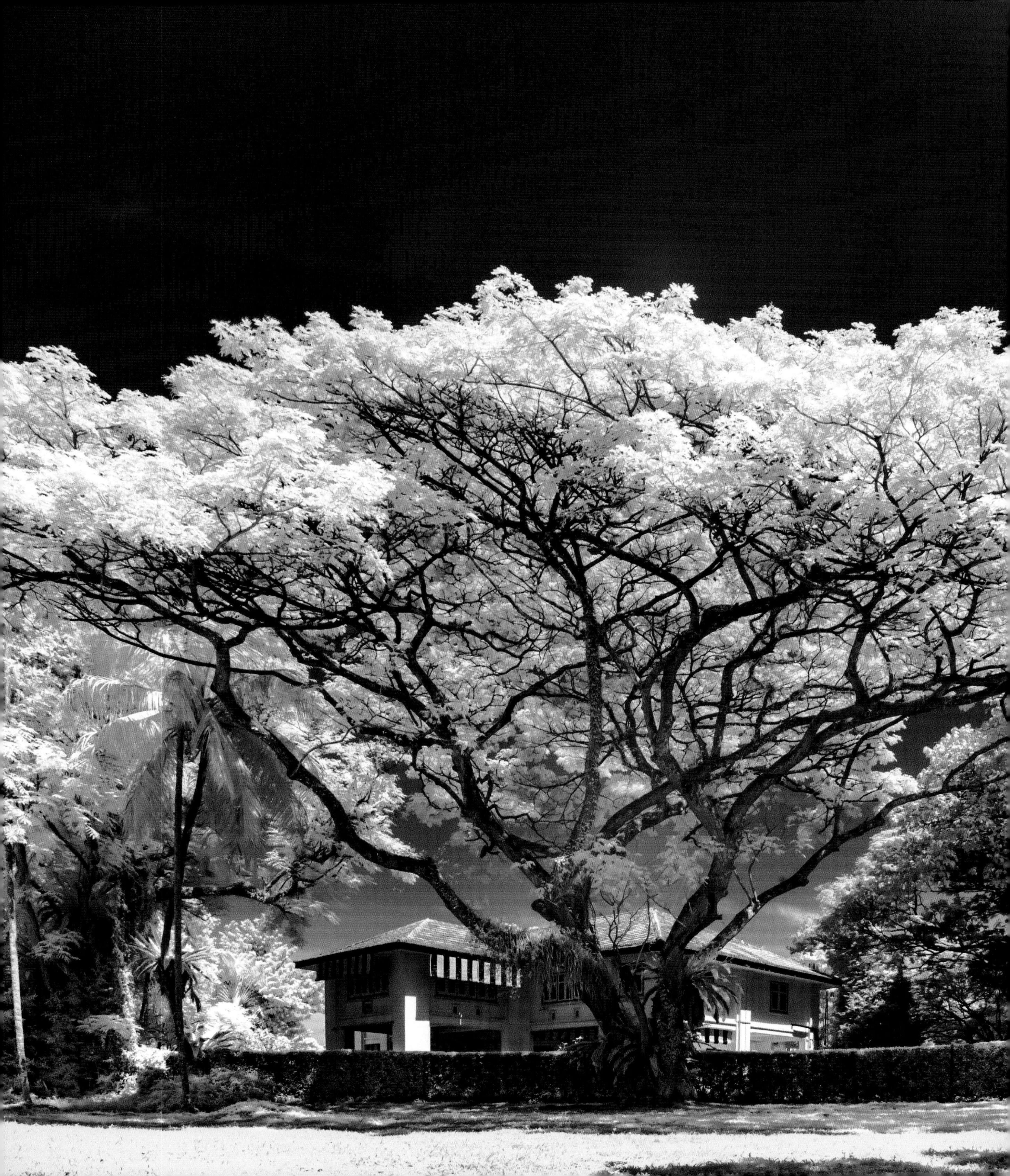

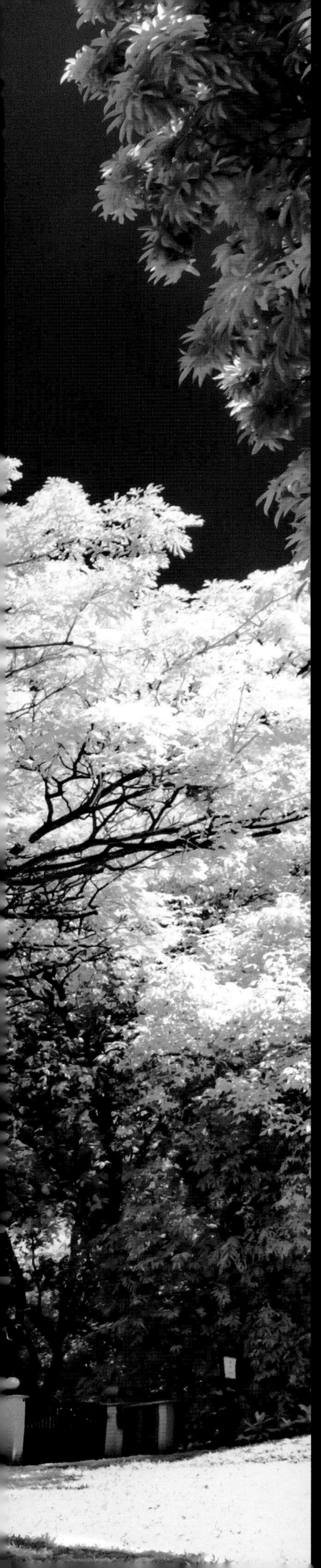

Samanea saman, Rain Tree

Sir Frederick Seton James, who eventually became the Governor of Grenada, lived here when he was the Colonial Secretary in Singapore between 1916-18.

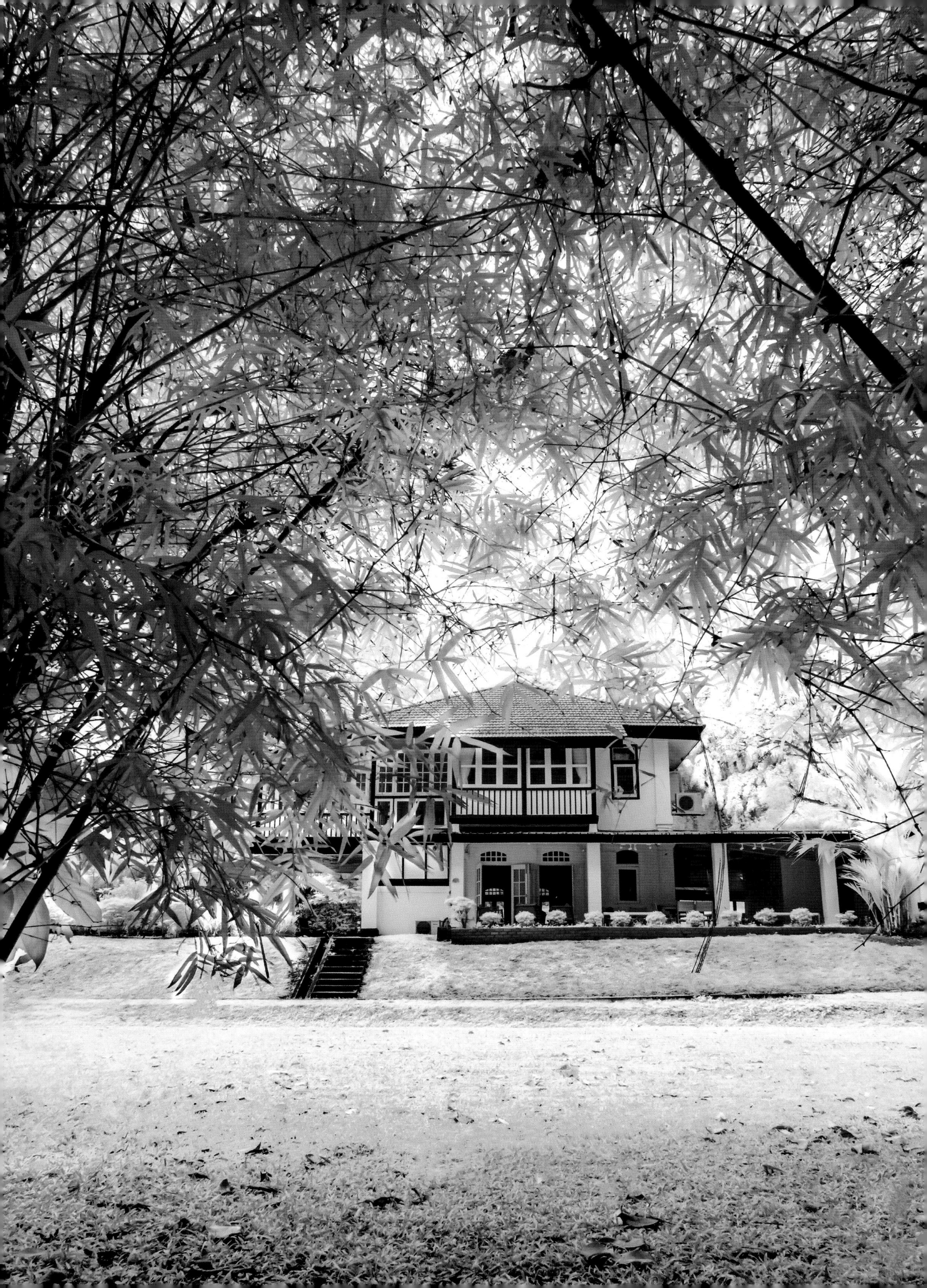

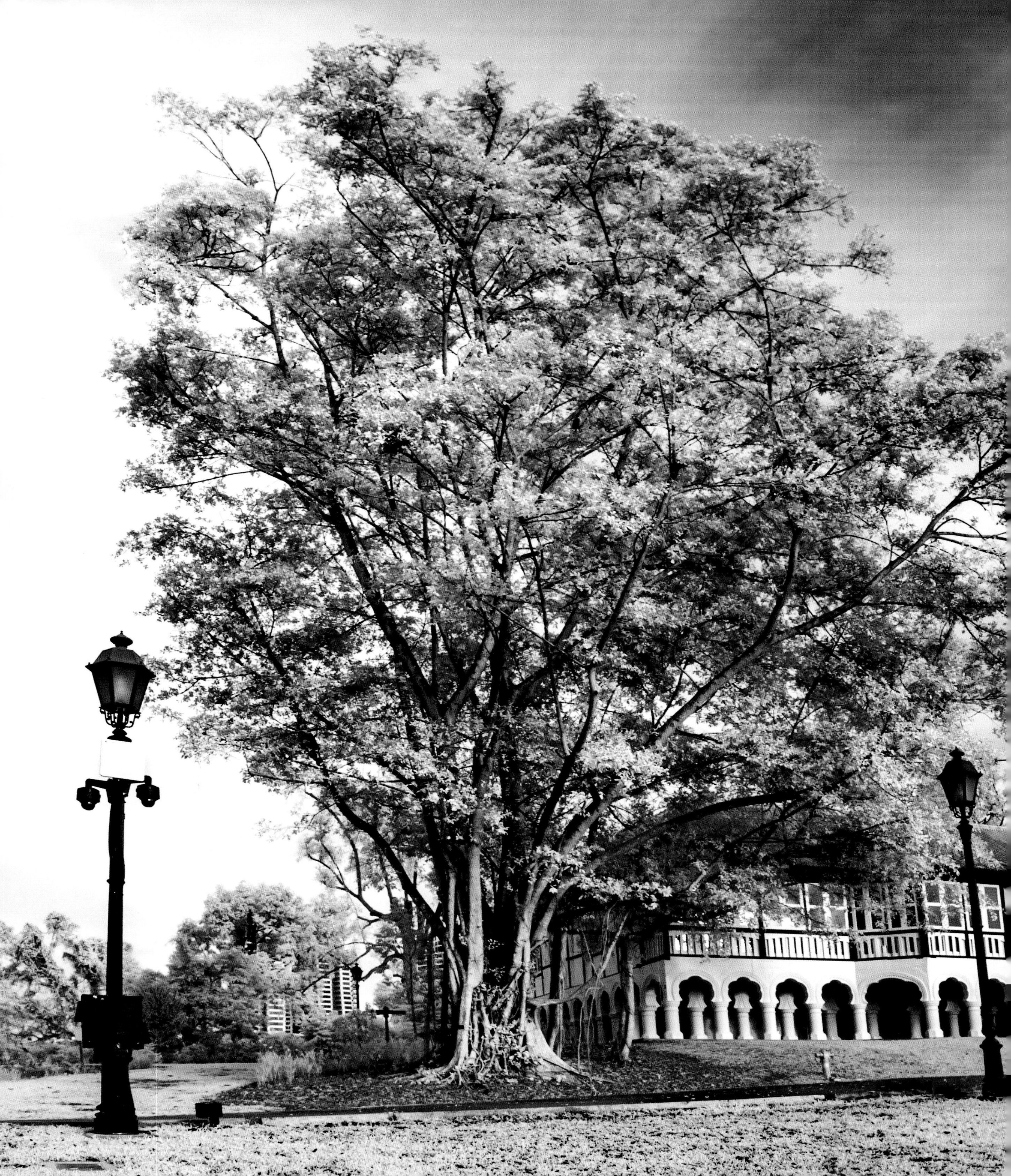

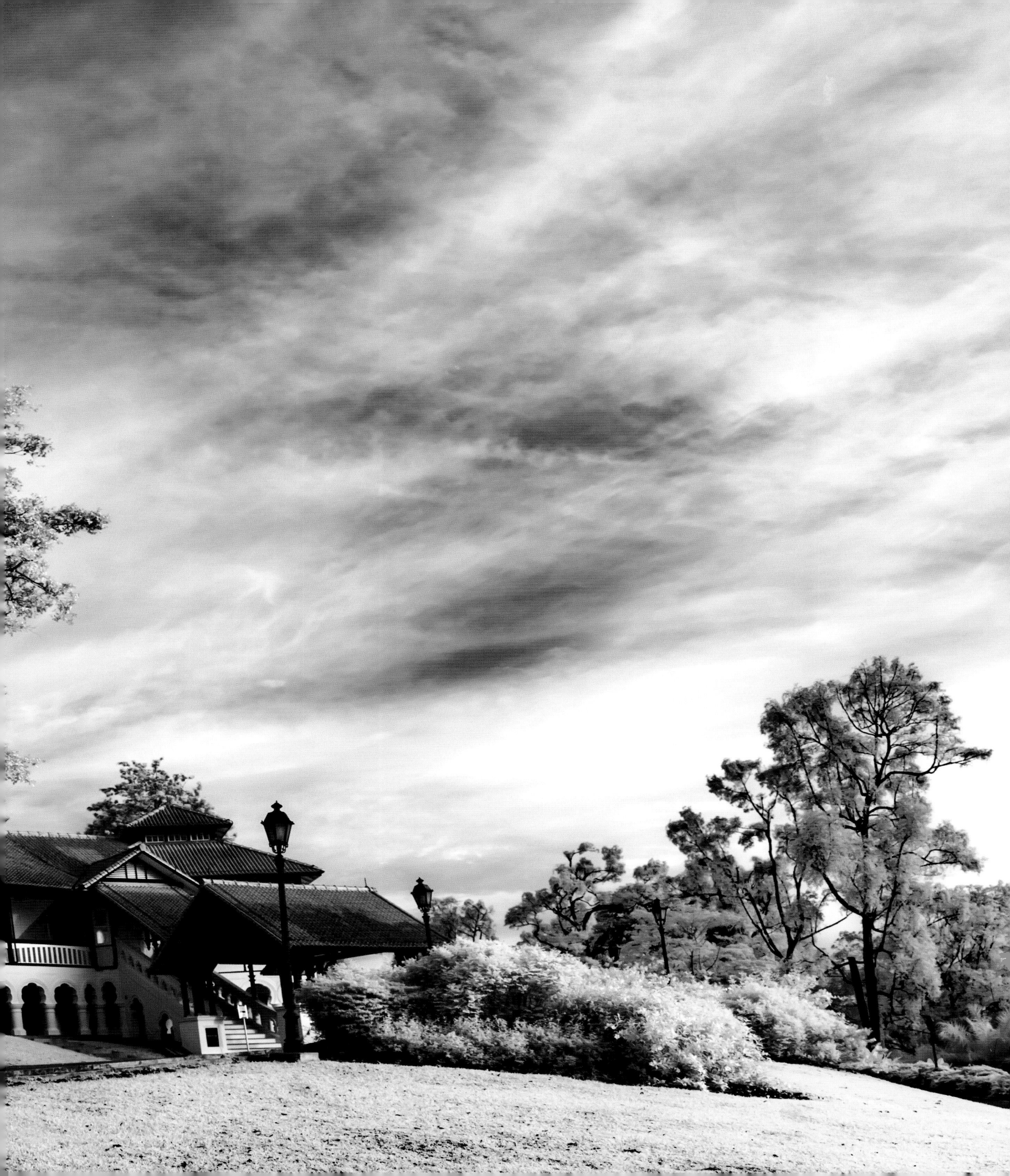

The houses at Orange Grove Road were designed by Swan & Mclaren and built in 1895. With the exception of a few buildings in Singapore that are not currently in residential use, according to Dr Julian Davison, these Orange Grove houses are probably the oldest houses in Singapore today that remain in residential use.

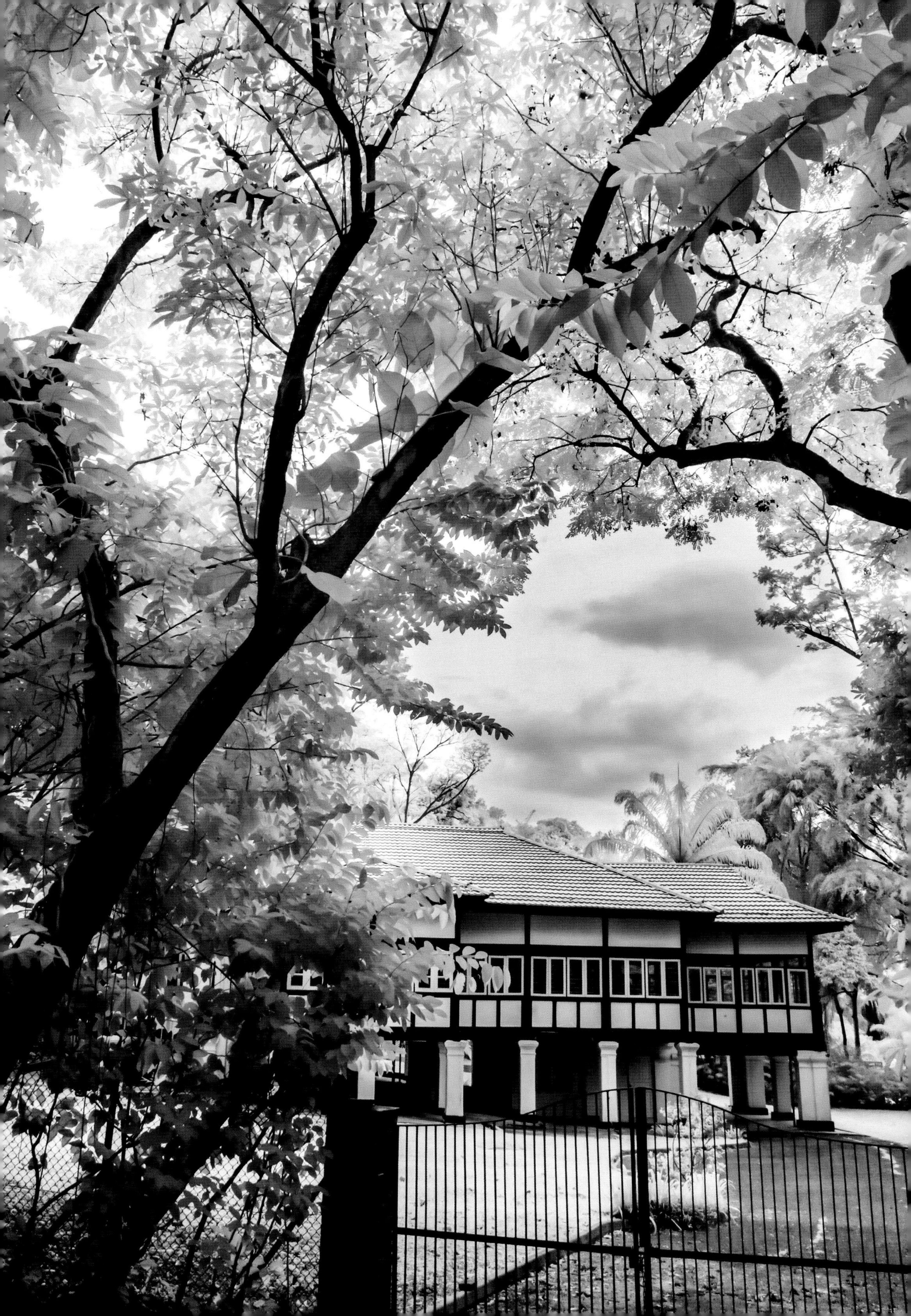

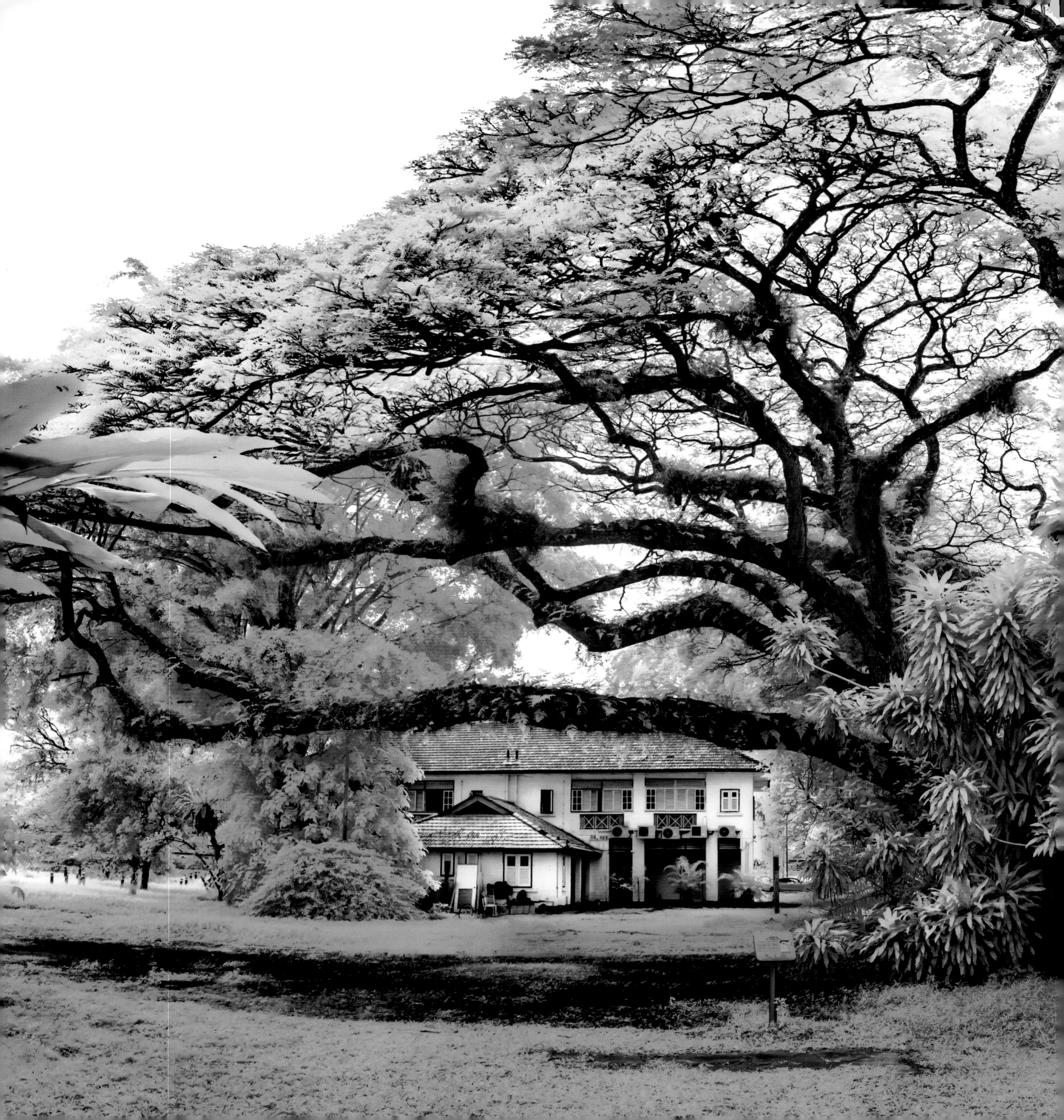

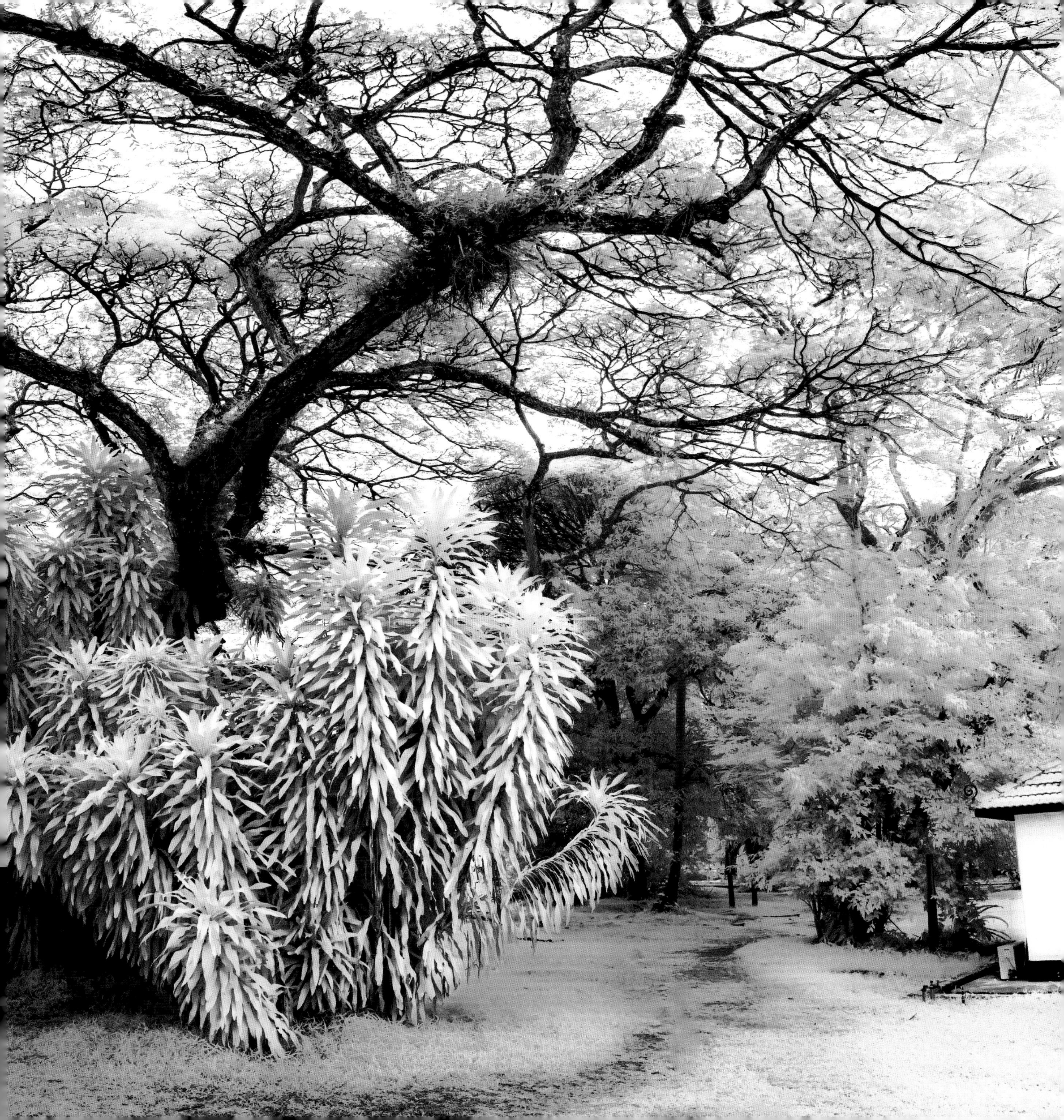

Singapore's Heritage Tree Program is a conservation initiative that aims to identify, protect and promote the appreciation of trees in Singapore that have significant cultural, historical, and ecological value.

Launched in 2001 by the National Parks Board the objective of the program includes the identification and documentation of heritage trees, the promotion of awareness and appreciation for these trees, and the development of conservation strategies to protect and preserve them. Once a tree is recognized as a heritage tree, it is accorded legal protection and conservation measures are put in place to ensure its preservation.

The program has become an important part of Singapore's national identity.

The trees shown on p. 14-15, 66-67 and 102-103 of this book are Heritage Trees.

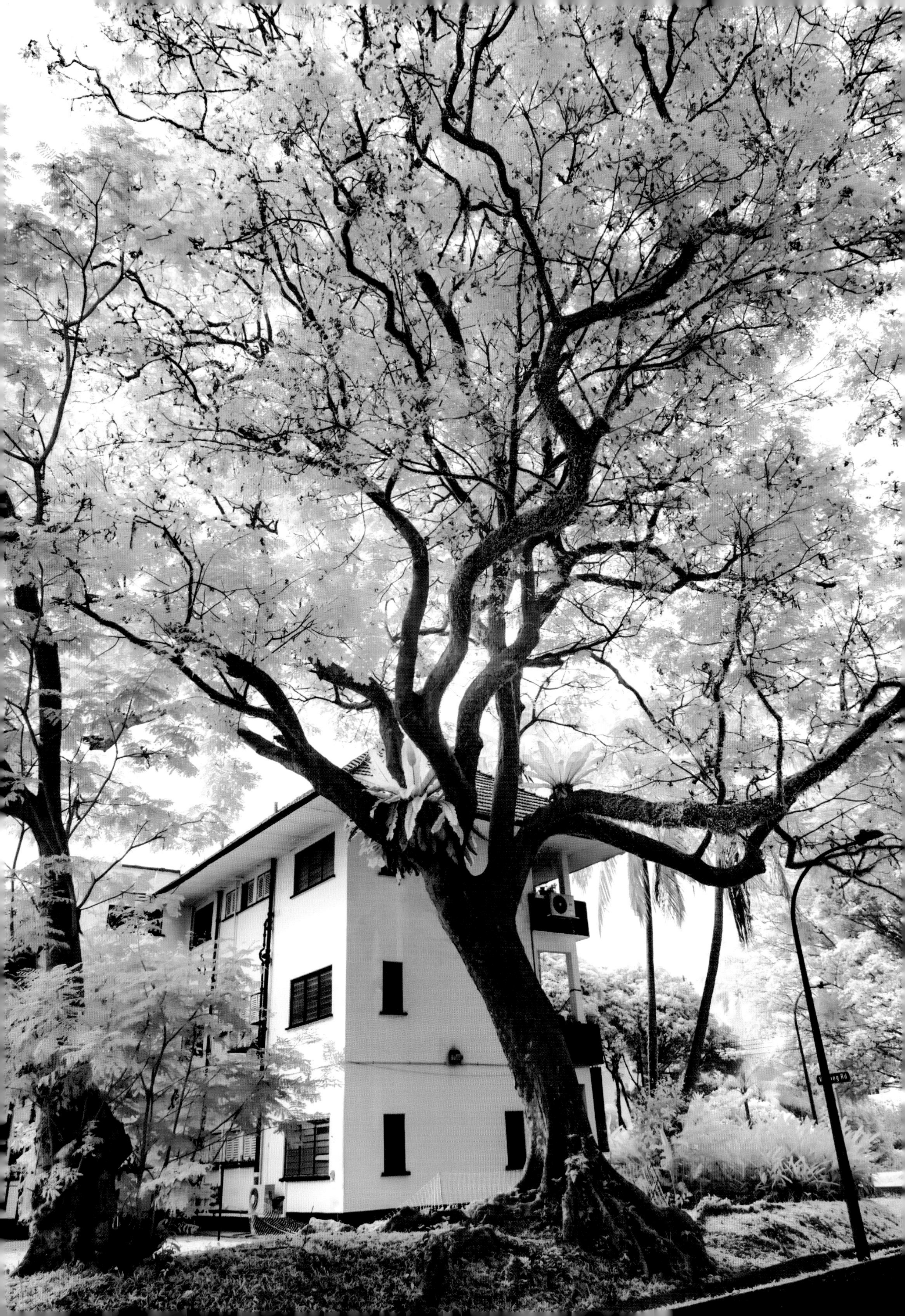

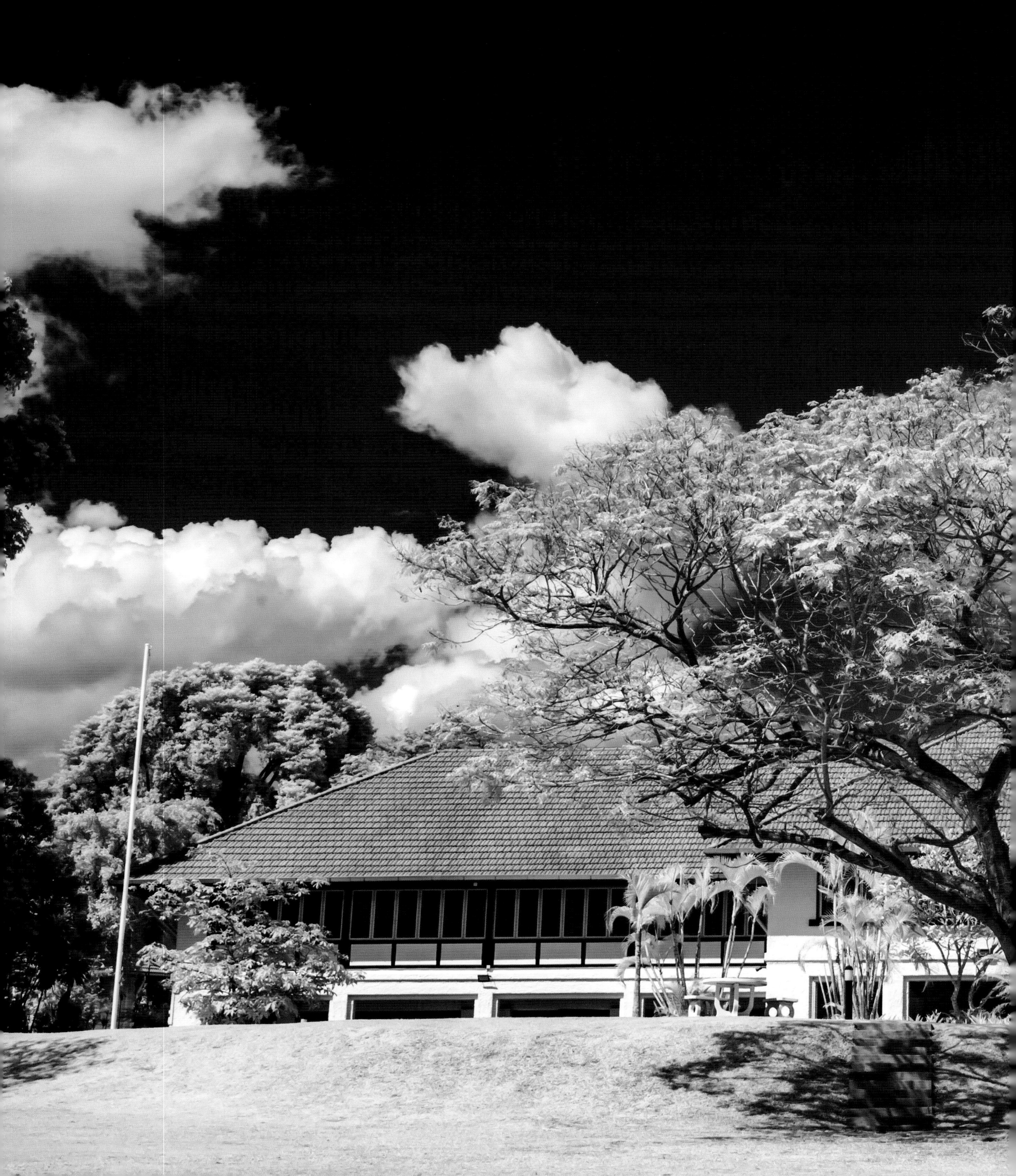

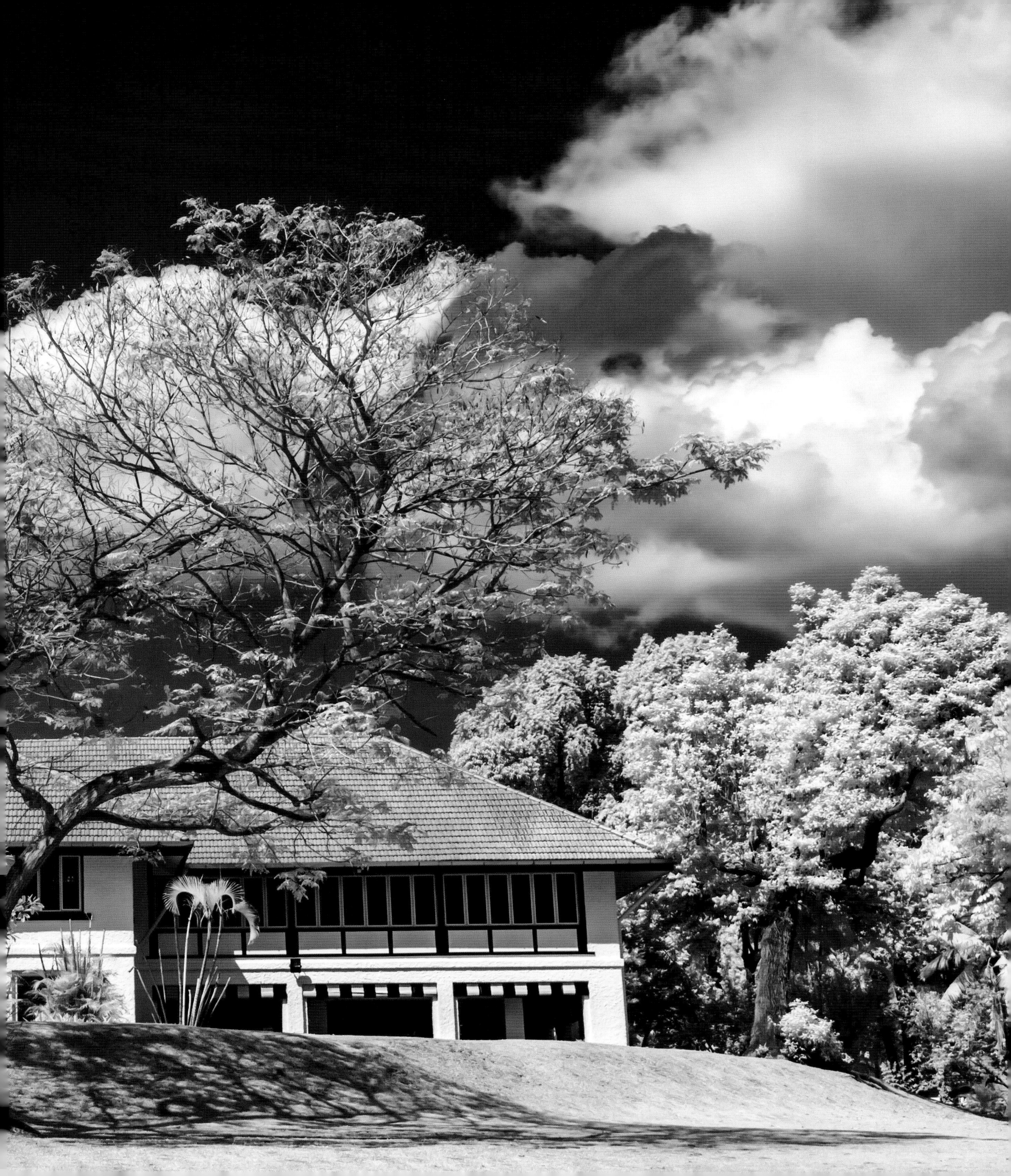

Betel nuts are sourced from the Areca palm and are believed to be one of the most popular mind-altering substances in the world. In Asia, it is popular to chew the nut; it gives people a buzz equivalent to drinking six cups of coffee.

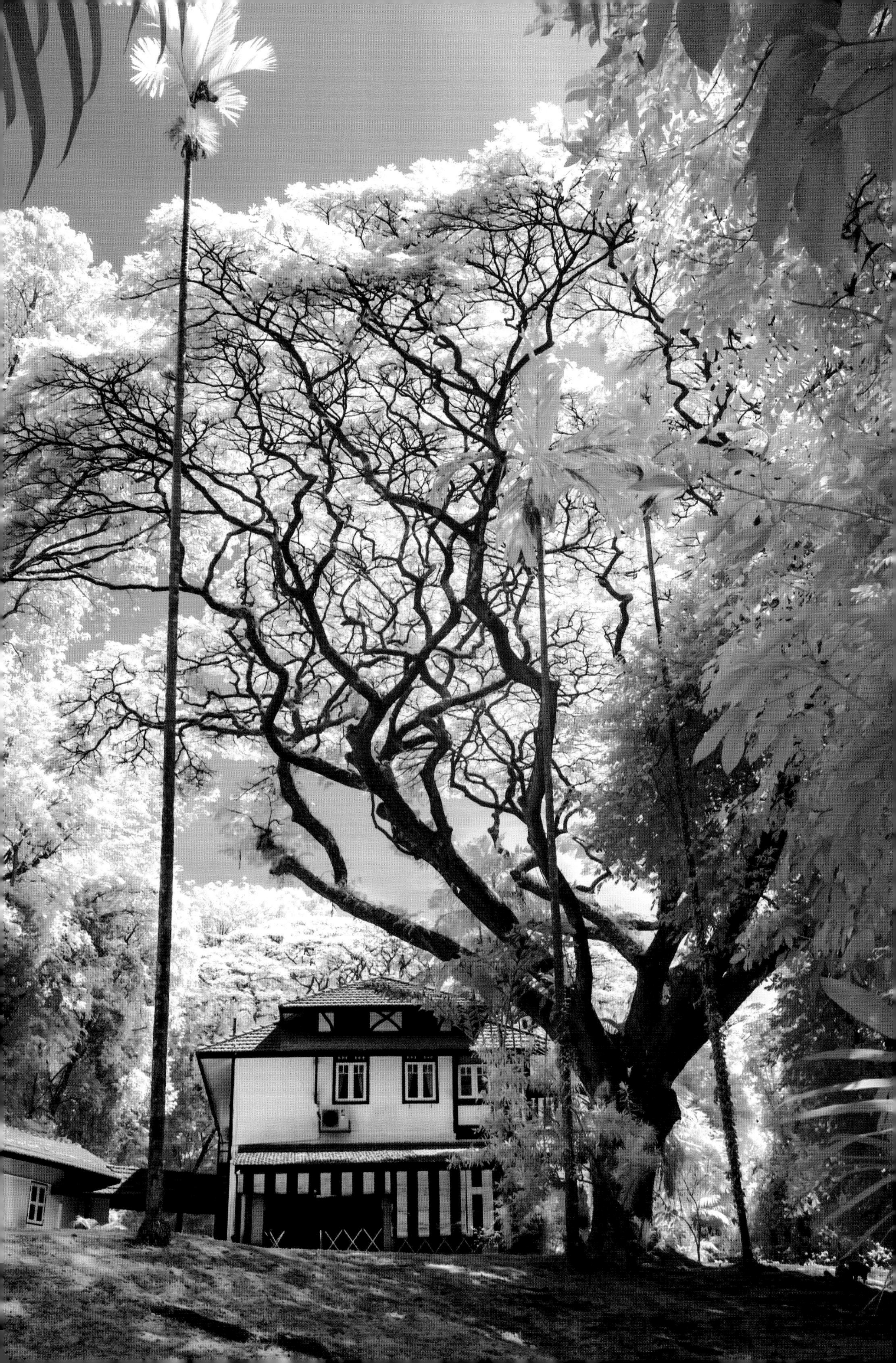

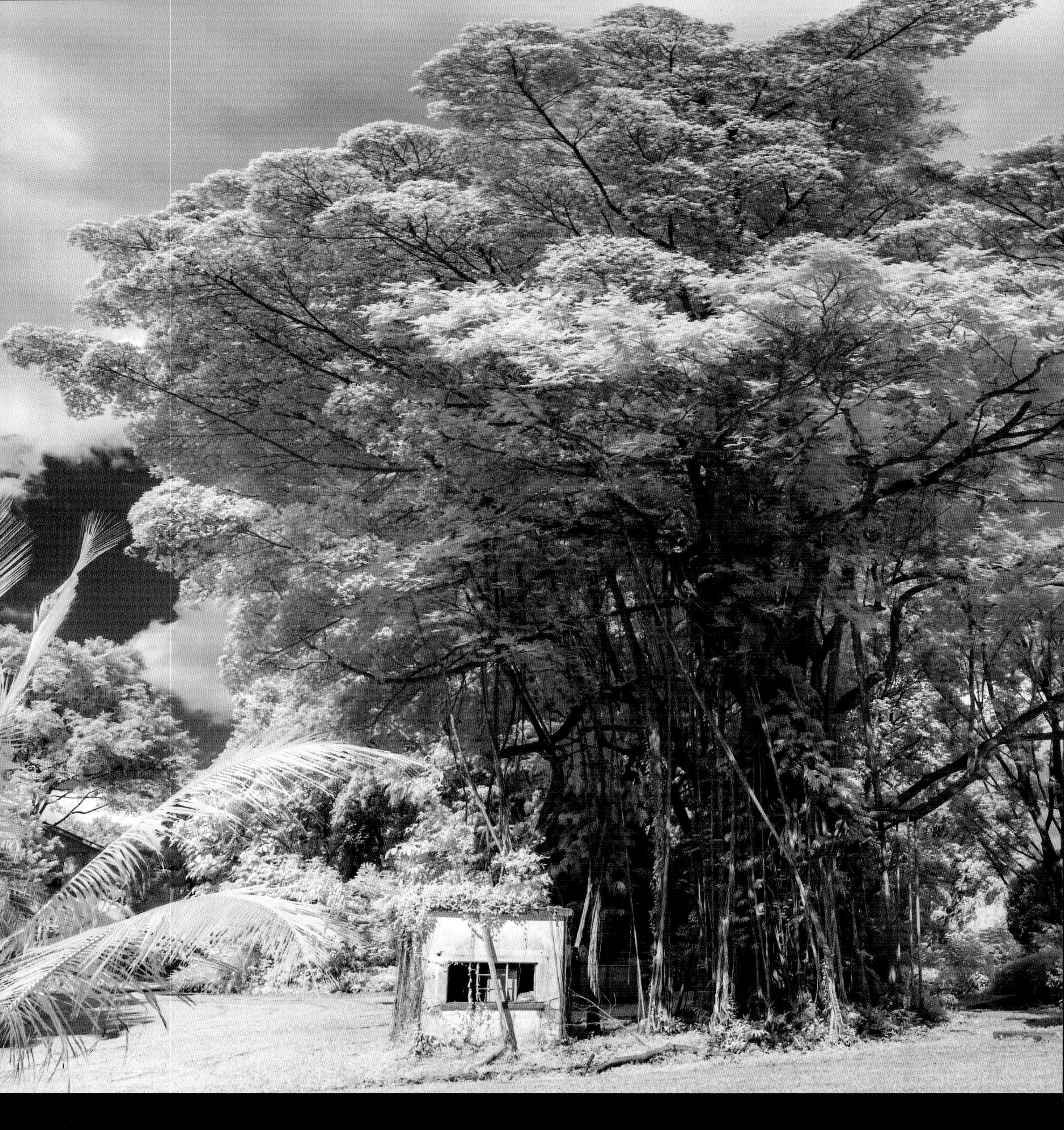

110 *Ficus benjamina*, Weeping Fig or Malayan Banyan

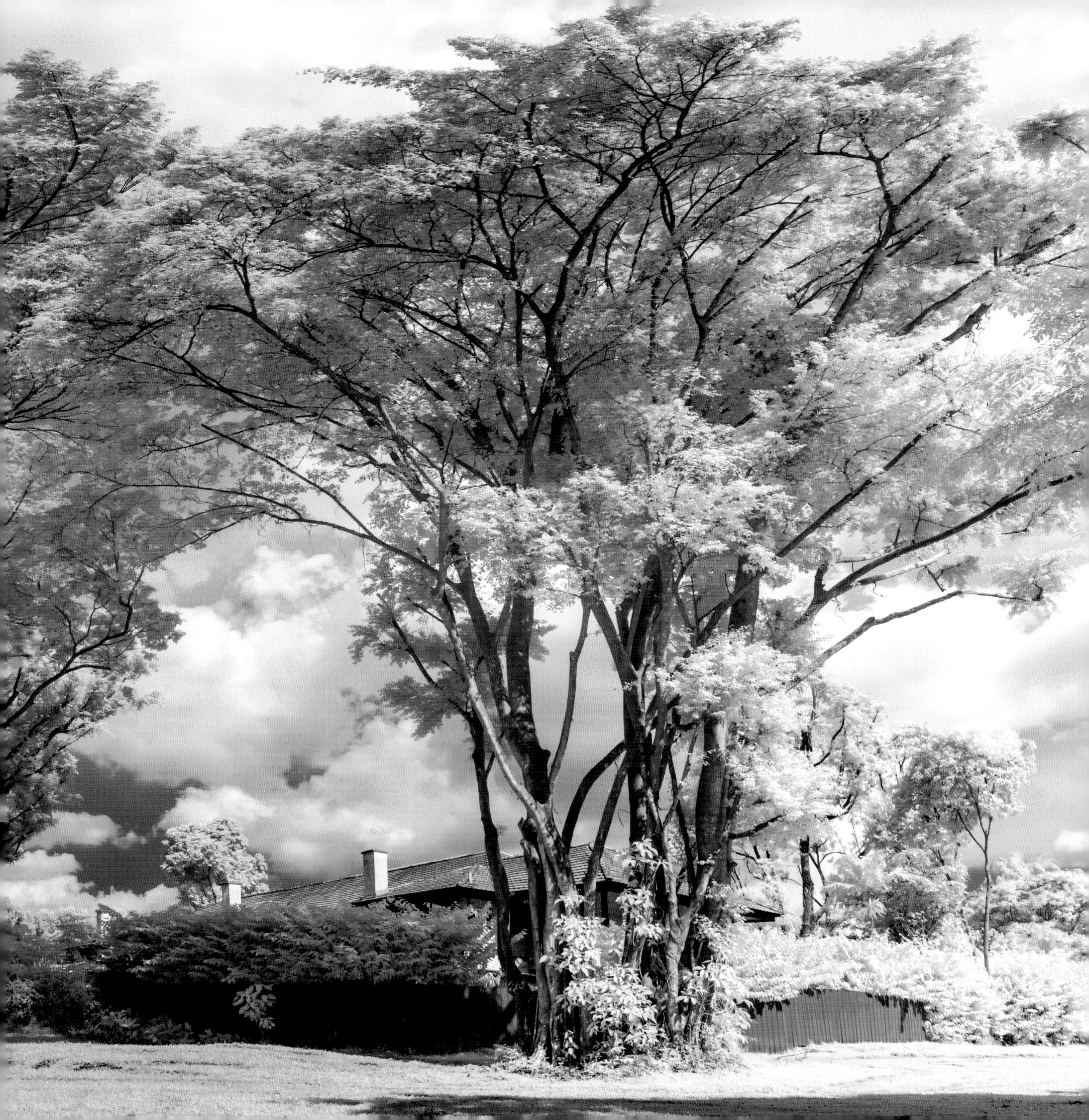

112 *Asplenium nidus*, Bird's Nest Fern growing on a Rain Tree

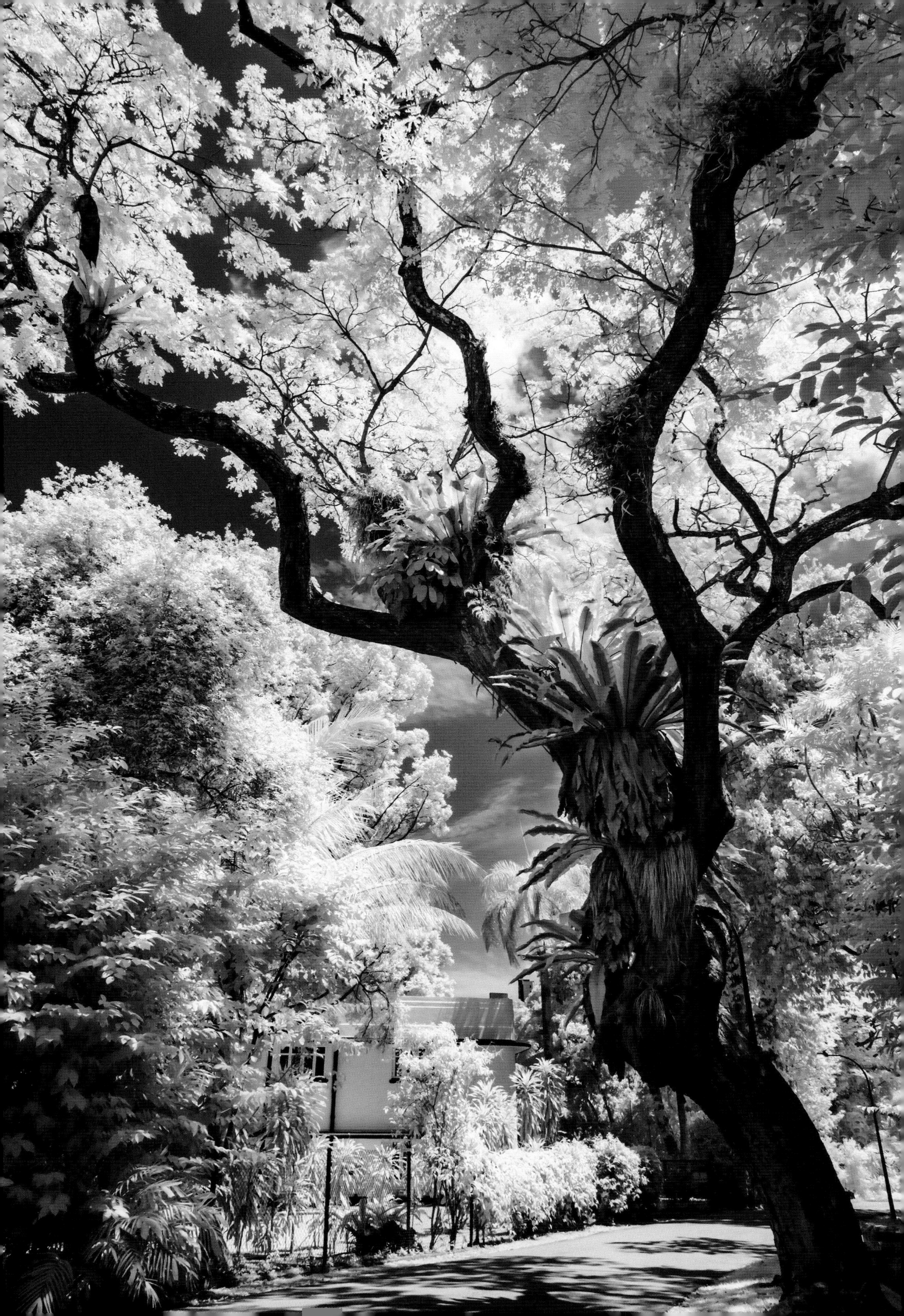

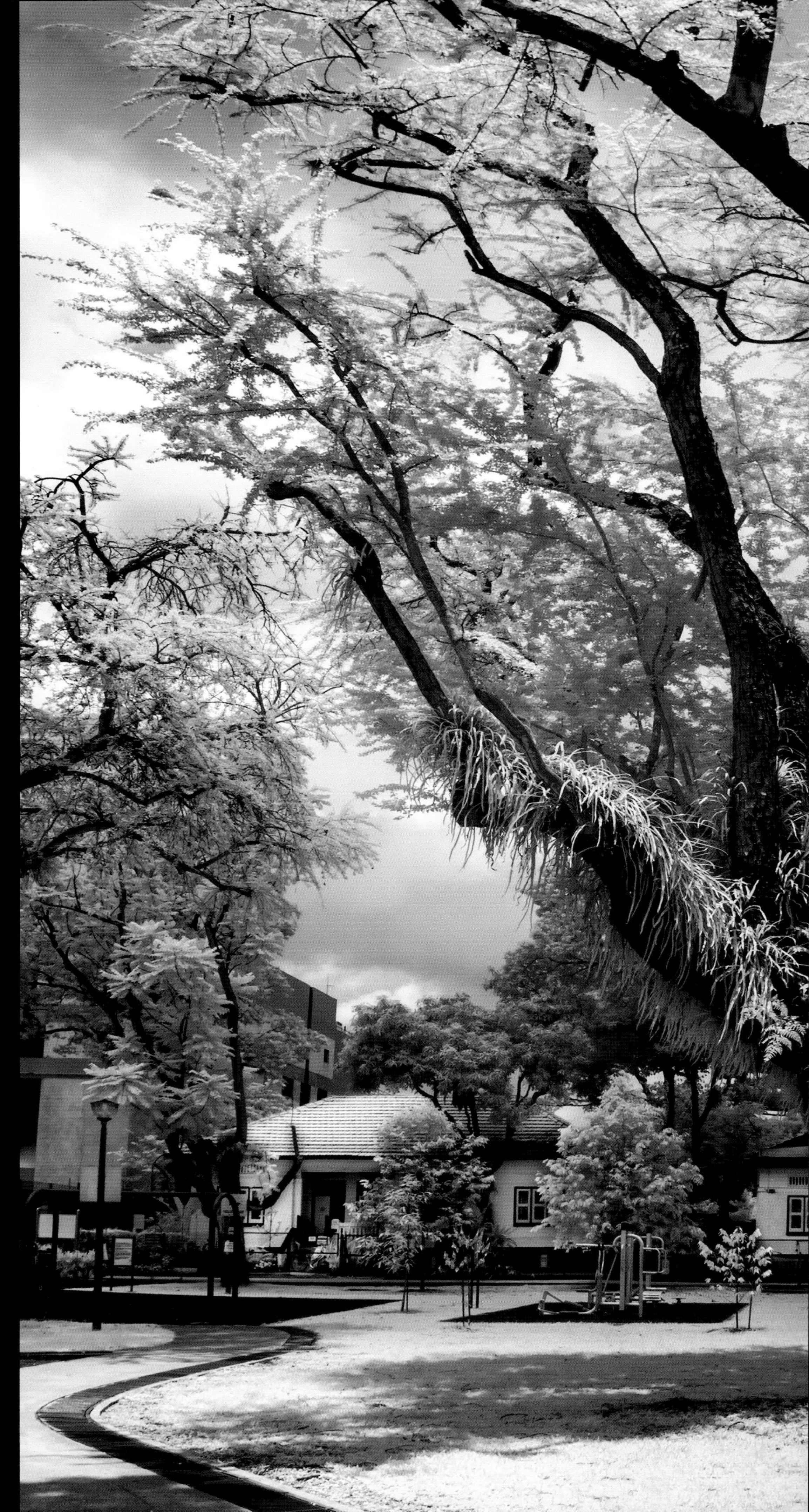

ecellobium dulce, Madras Thorn

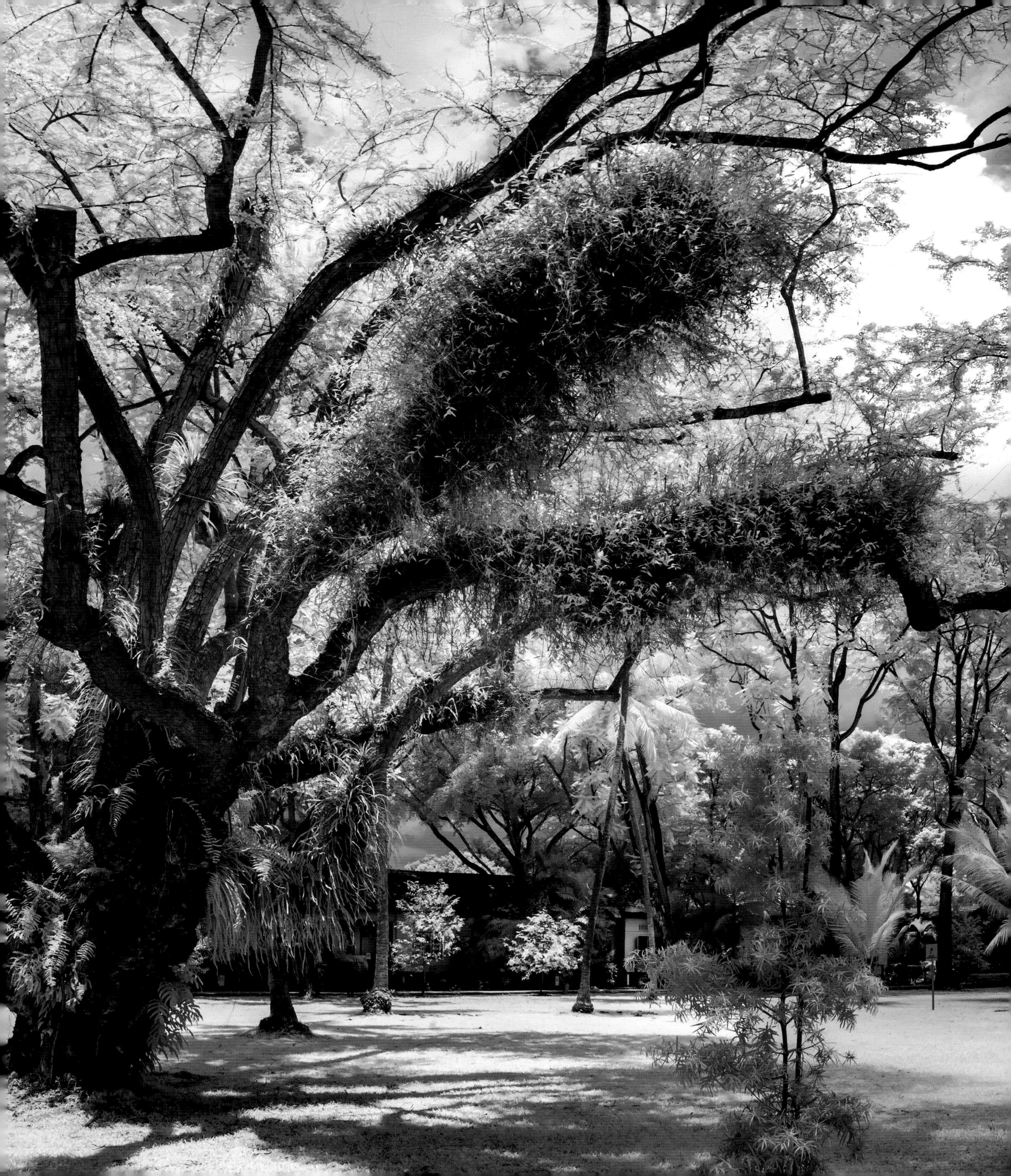

The Traveler's Palm is used as the emblem of Raffles Hotel, Singapore.

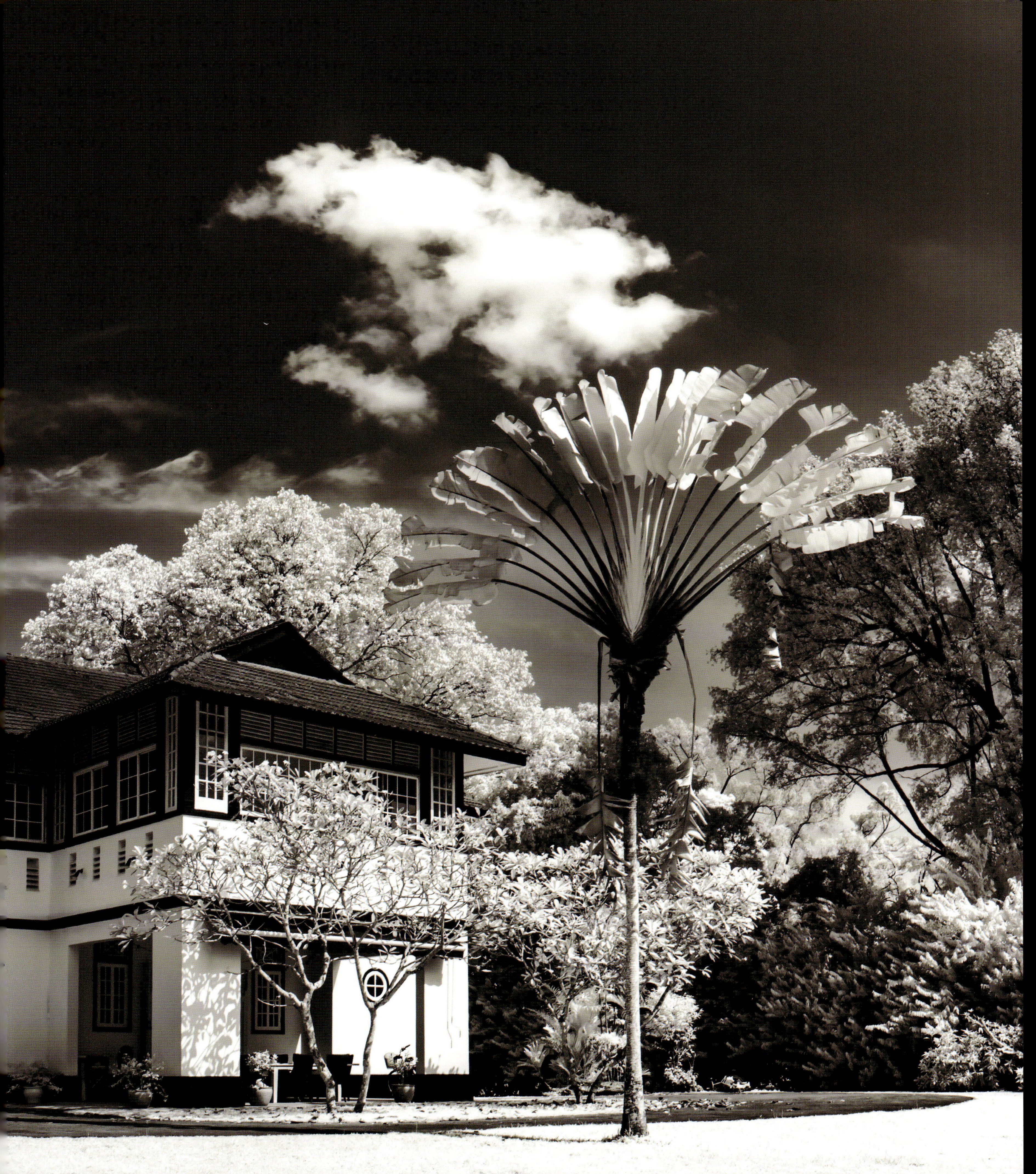

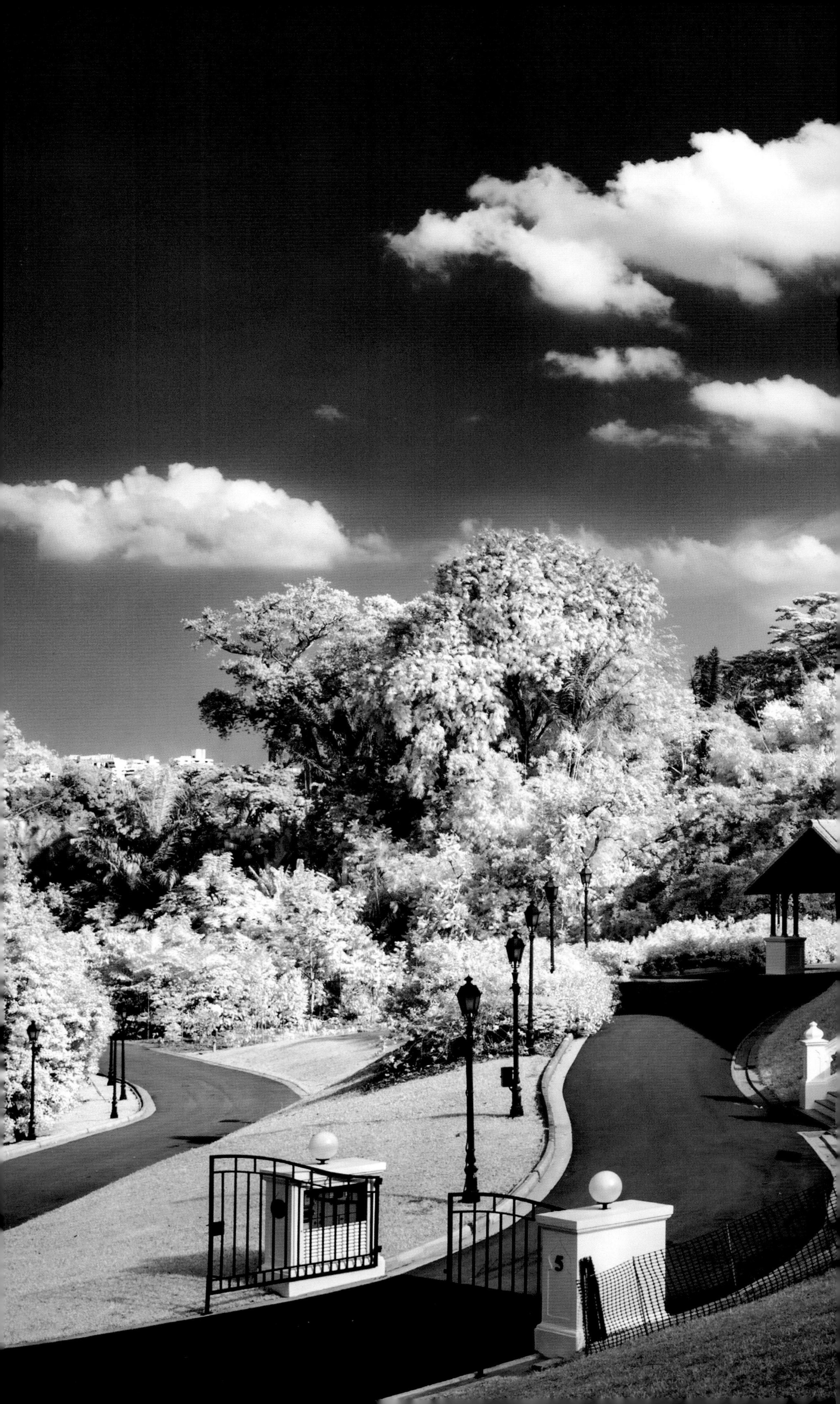
5

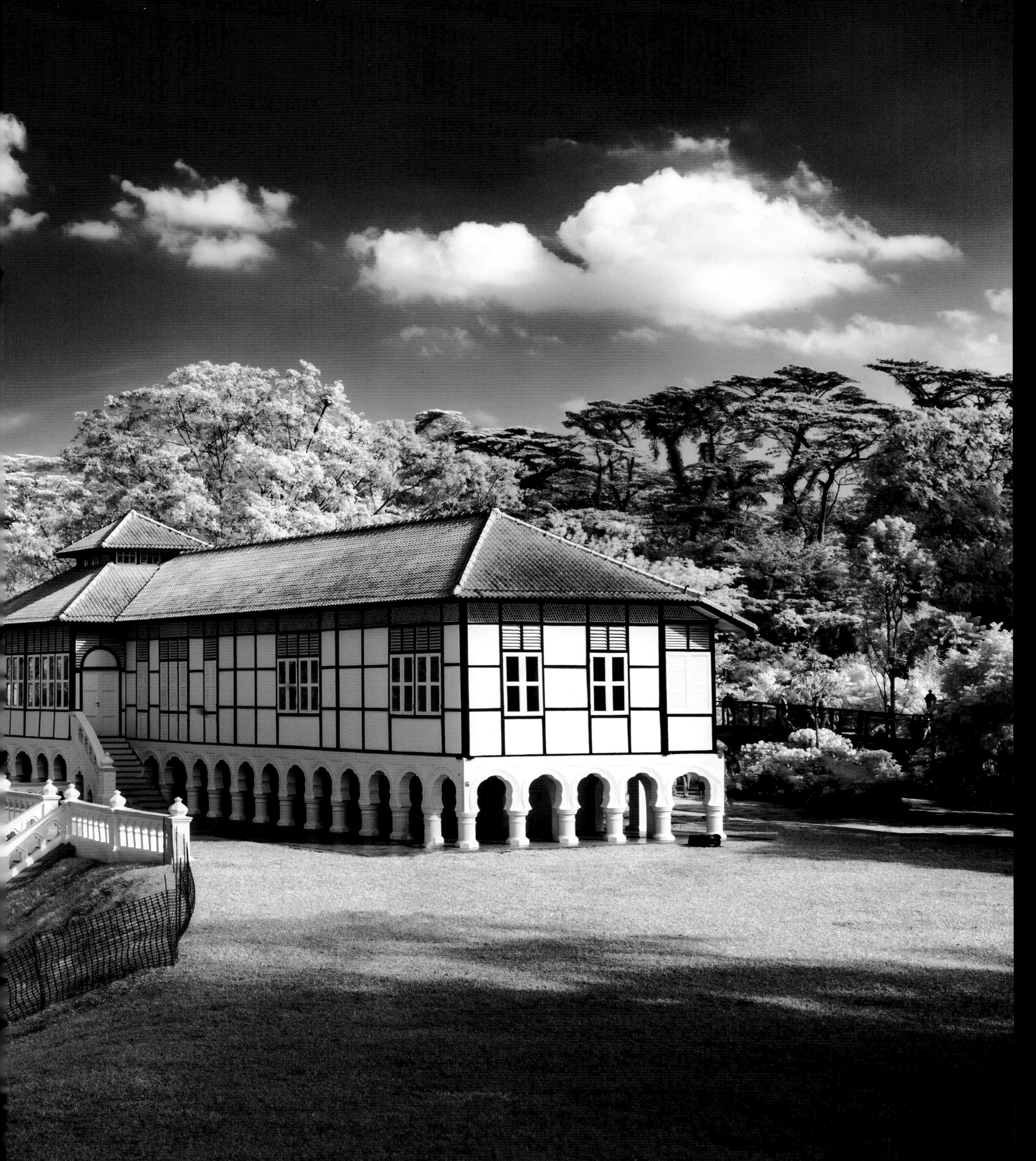

"Named after an important victory in the second Anglo-Sudanese war (1881-1899), Mr. Burkinshaw's bungalow represented another radical departure from the typical nineteenth-century Singapore house....

Perhaps the most unusual thing about Atbara, though, was an almost complete absence of verandahs such as one might normally have expected in a contemporary bungalow."

Dr Julian Davison, Swan & McLaren
- A Story of Singapore Architecture.

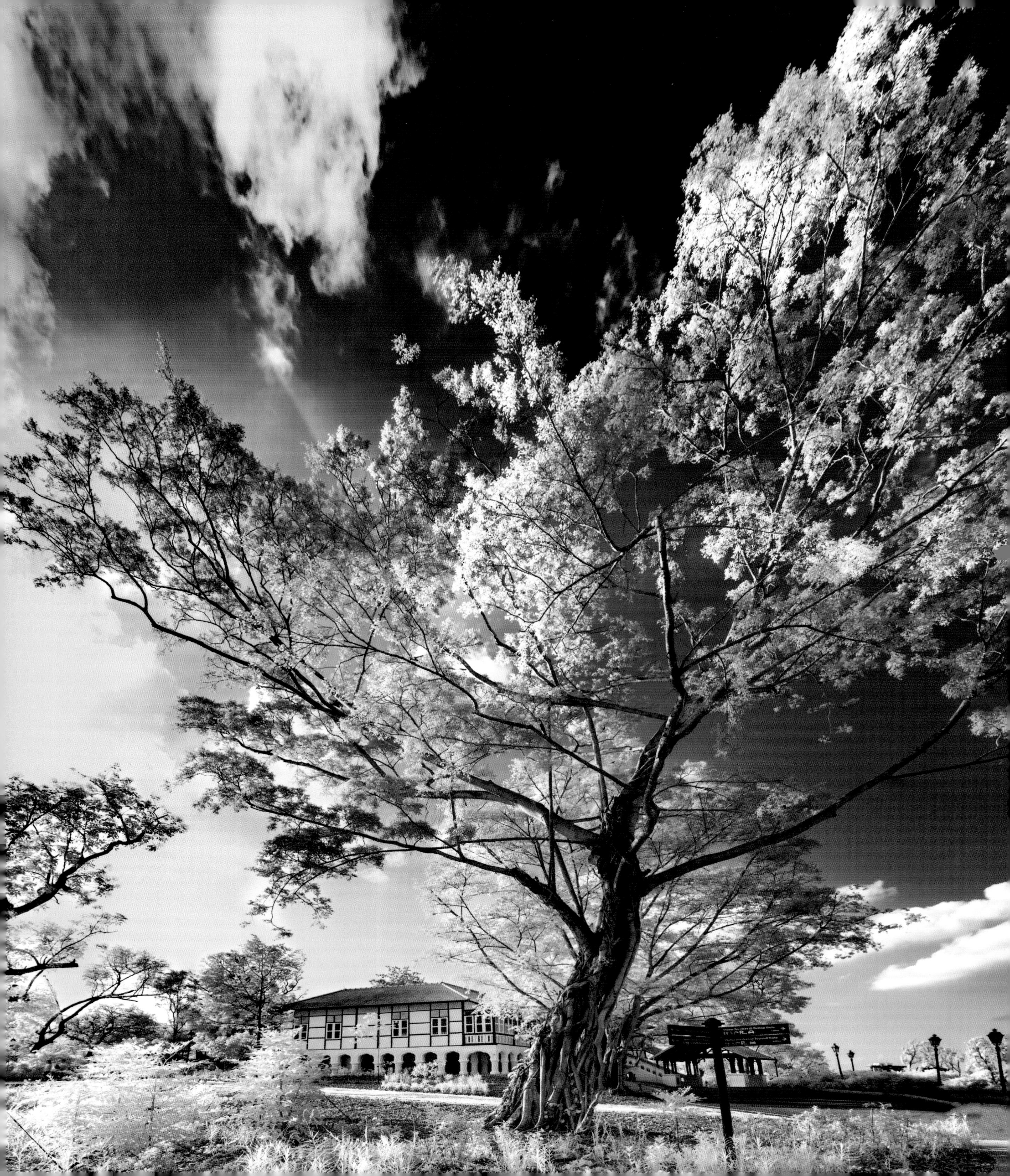

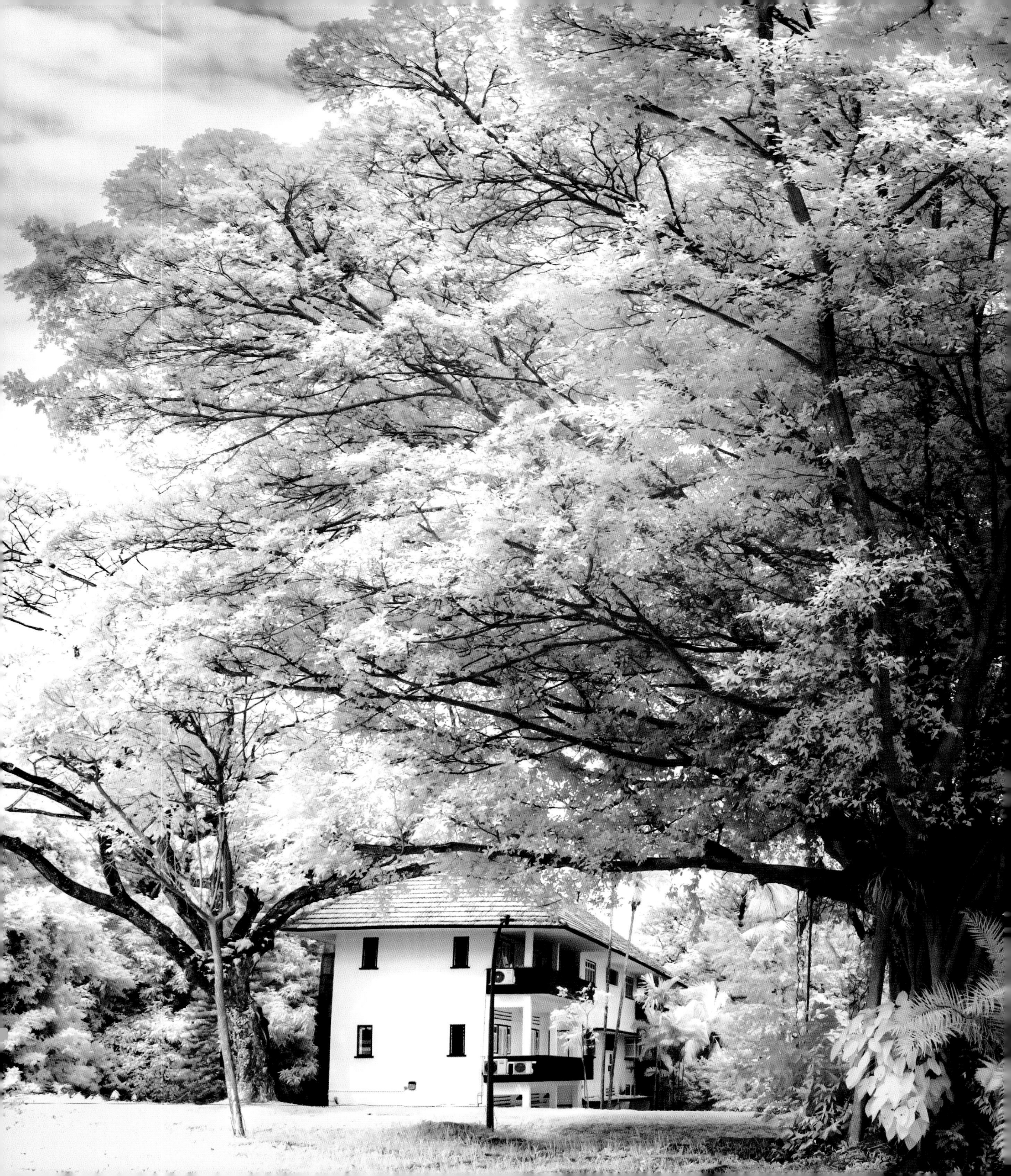

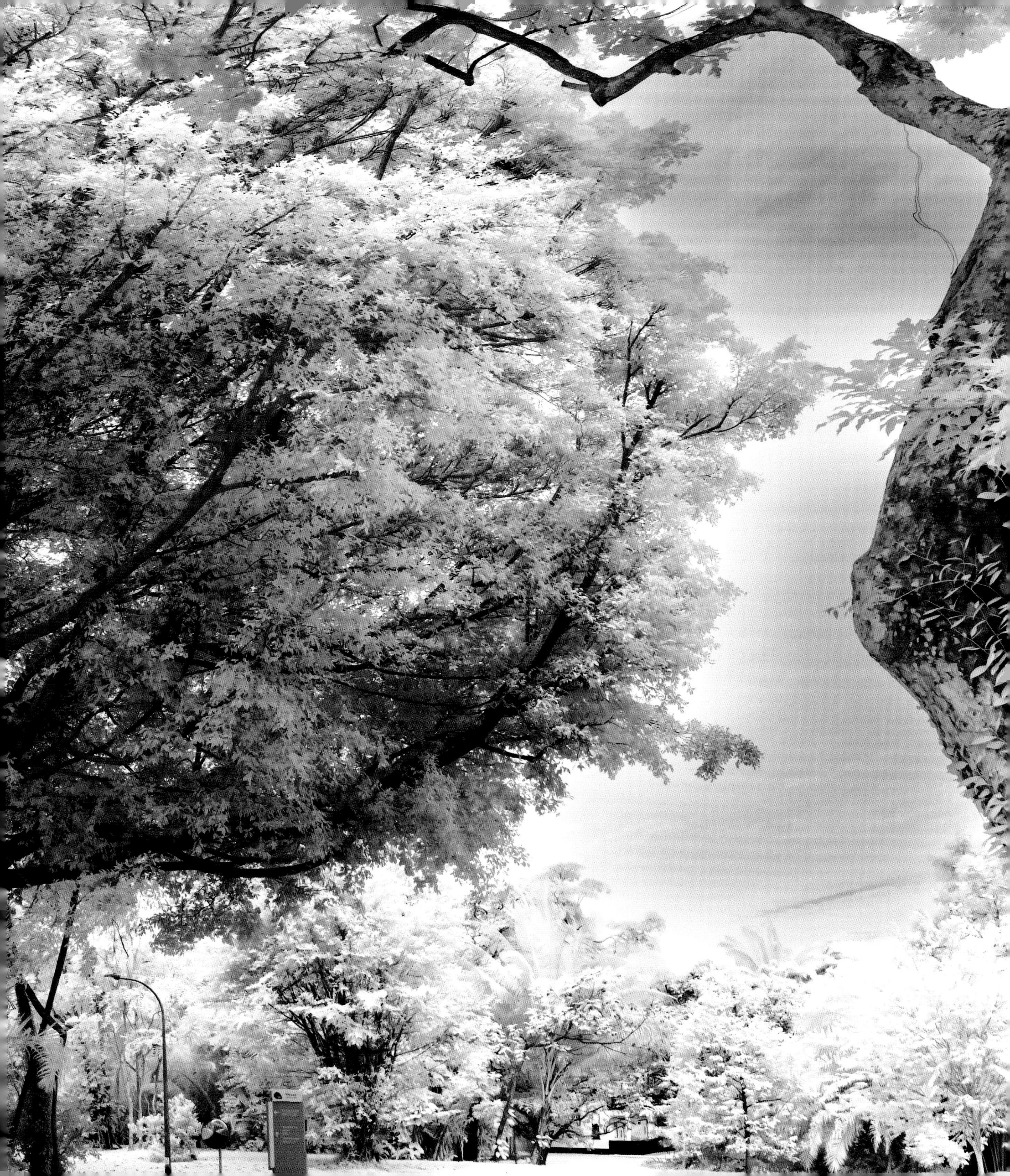

124 *Elaeis guineensis,* Oil Palm

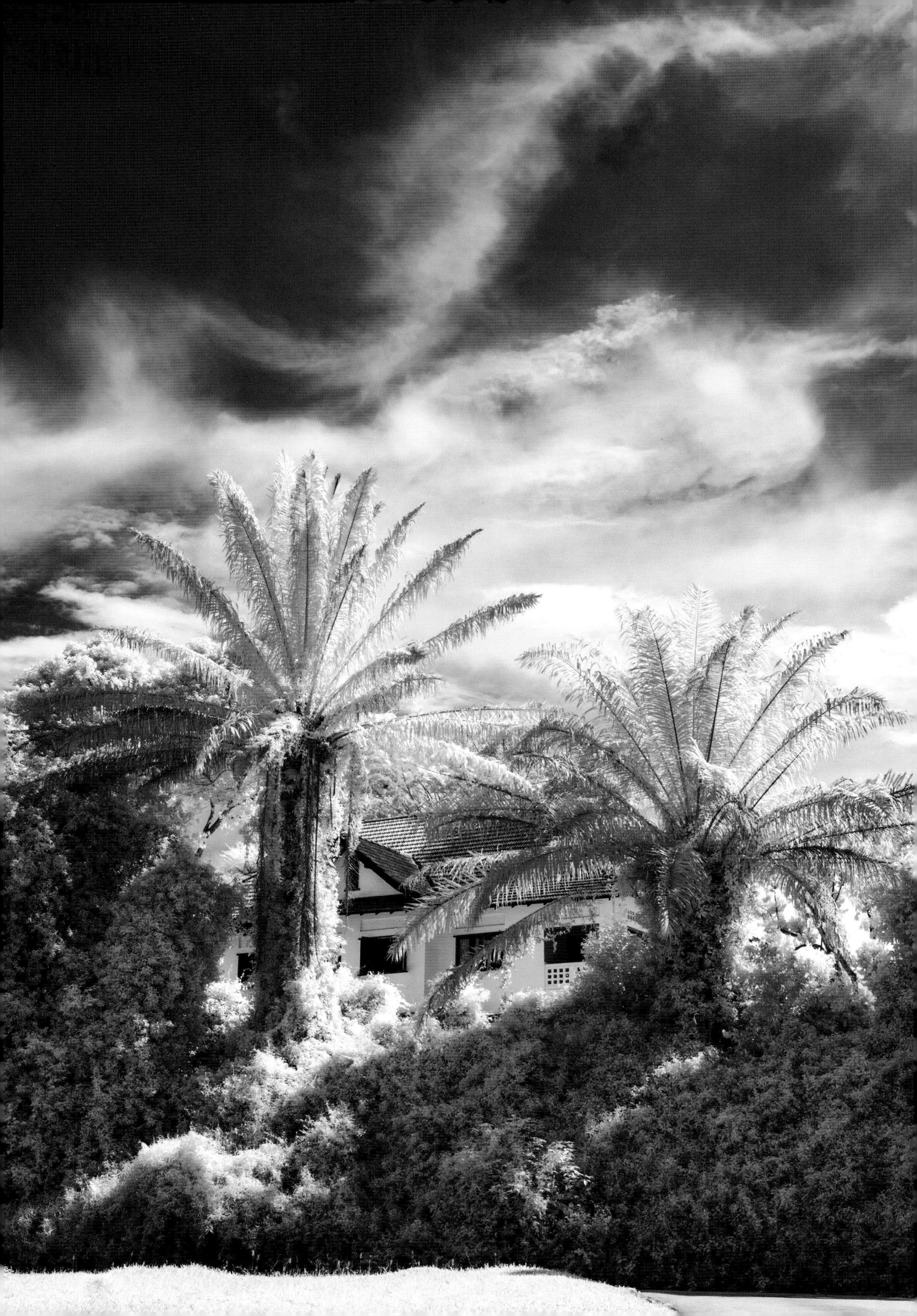

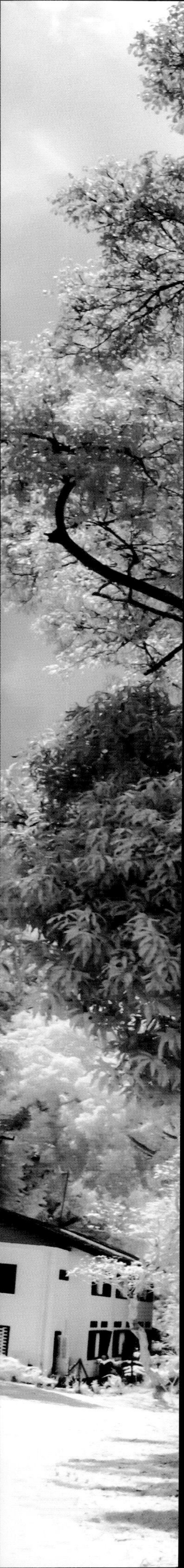

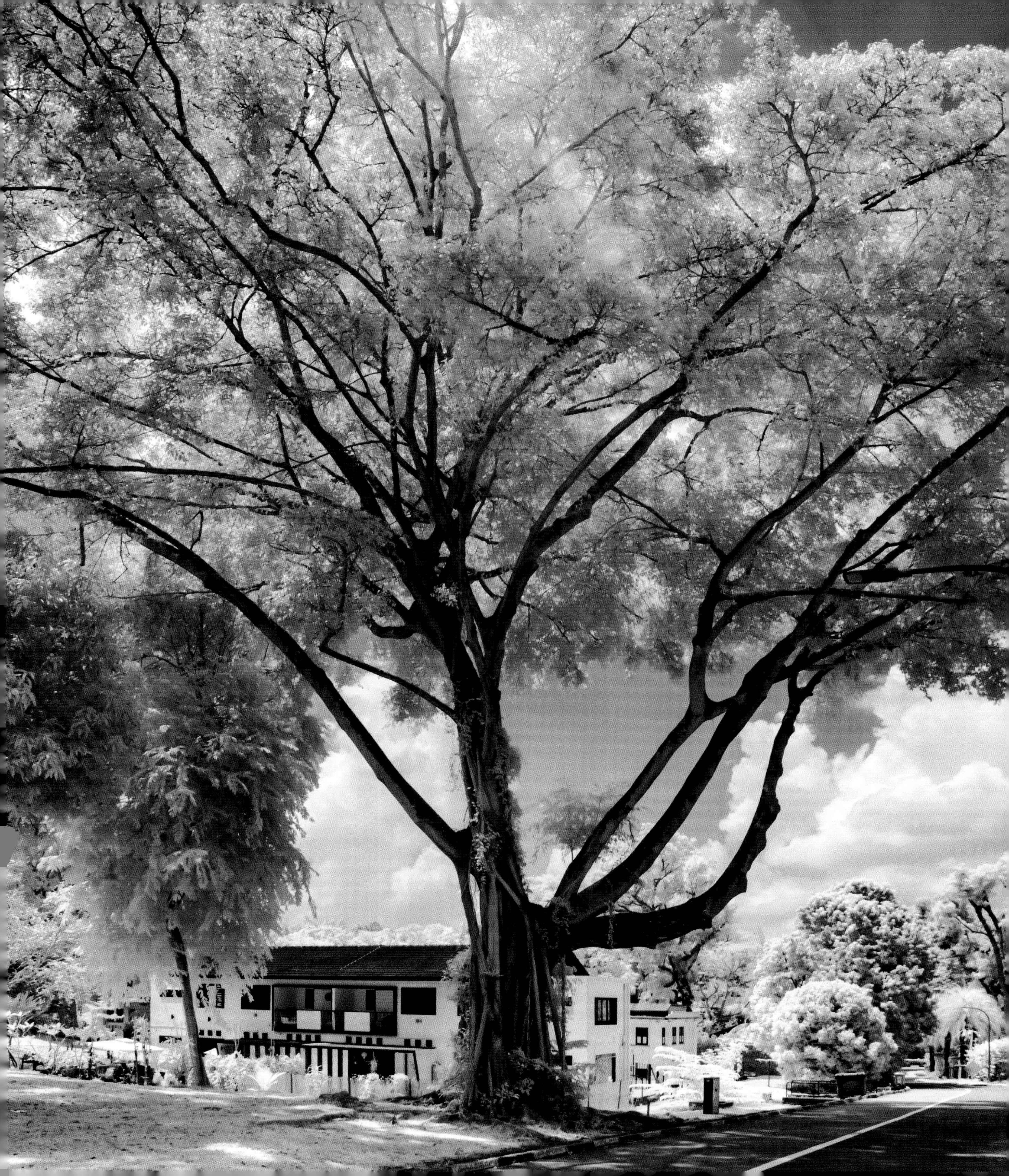

Alexandra Park was at the centre of the Singapore mutiny of 1915 which was triggered when rumours spread falsely within the 5th Light Infantry that they were going to be sent to Mesopotamia to fight the Turks during World War I.

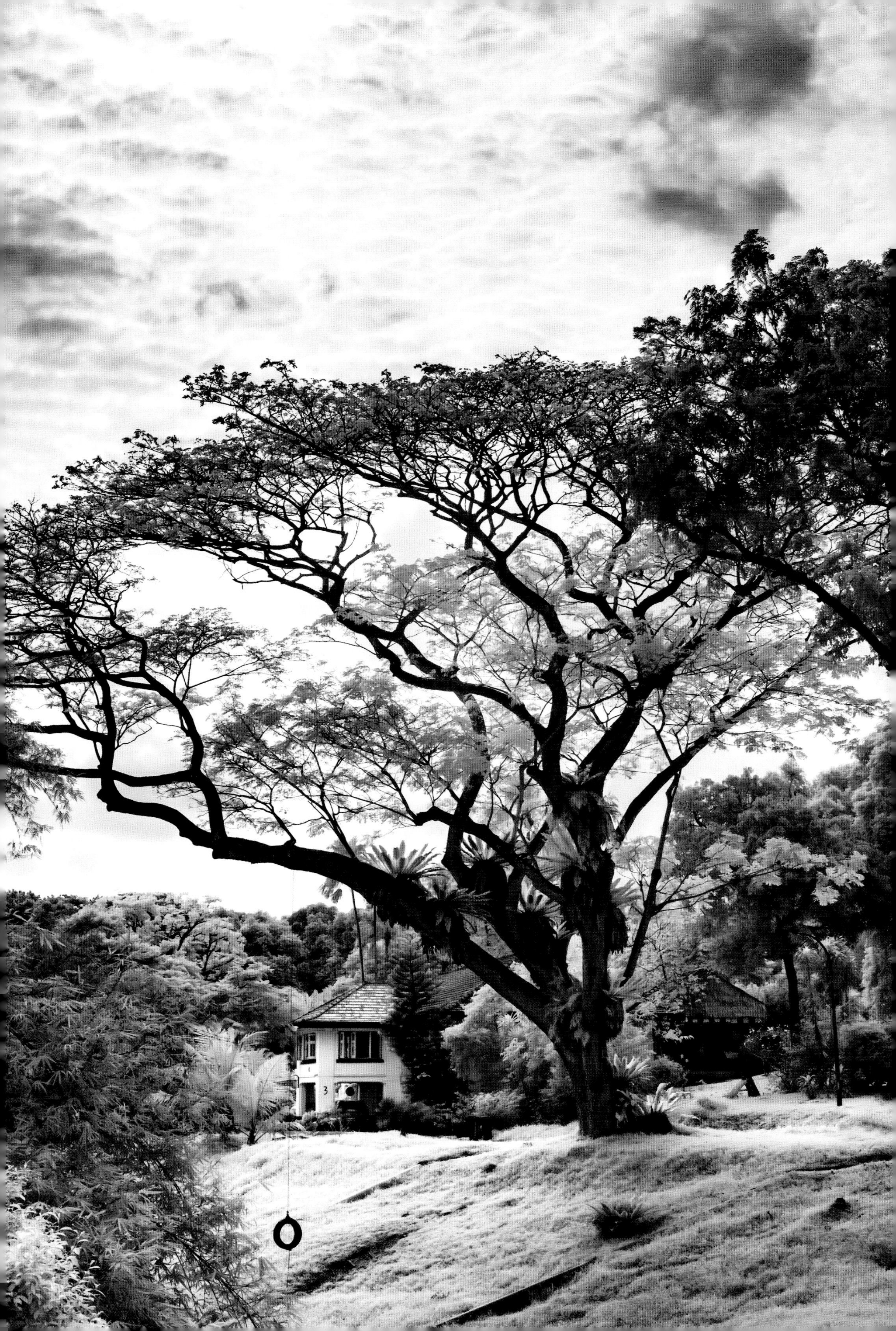

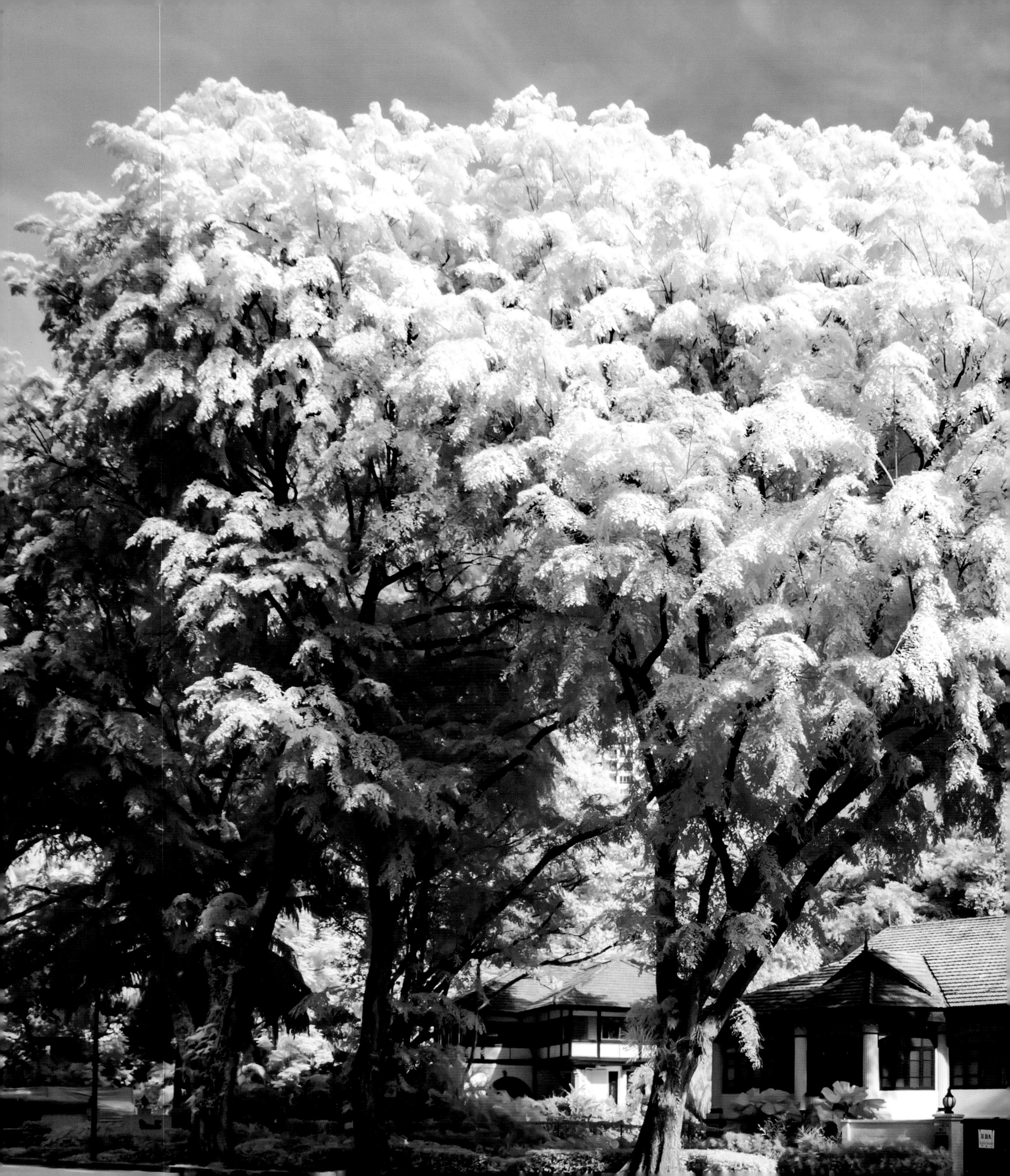

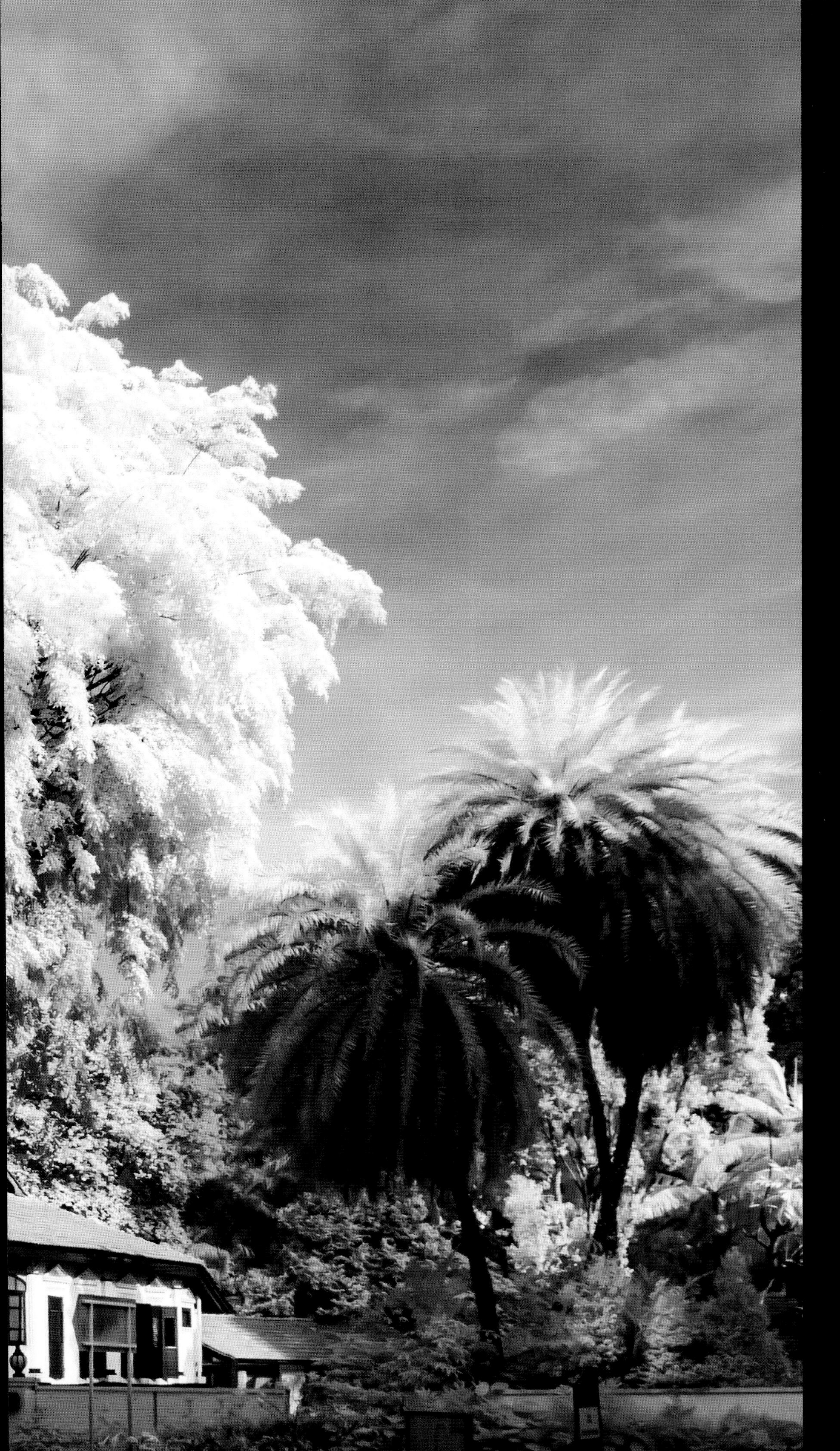

Pterocarpus indicus, Angsana

Acknowledgements

This book would not have been possible without the generosity of the many residents who opened their homes to me and shared their experiences of living in their black and white houses. Thank you for your encouragement of my project, for sharing your connections of others who, in turn, also supported my project. My experience was all the more rewarding for meeting you. I drew inspiration from your passion and love for your homes.

A few of you have gone out of your way to help me with my project and deserve a special mention. Thank you Linda Ying, Farhana Sharmeen, Sian Morgan Jones, Barbara Voskamp, Jane Iyer, Elango Velautham, Dan Perera and Dr Julian Davison.

I would also like to thank the many photographers who have directly or indirectly inspired me to continue to grow and develop my own skills. I have learnt from each and every one of you and no doubt, will continue to learn and develop.

My heartfelt gratitude to my wife Fahima, who has been my greatest supporter as well as my greatest critic. She continues to push me to be the best photographer that I can be and, no doubt, I am what I am because of her. My thanks also to my daughters Anoushka and Ariana, who sacrificed their time with Daddy during many weekends over two years, allowing me to disappear for hours at a time for this project. I am blessed for having a family who indulges my passions. You make me a better person.

The Black & White Project -Unseen Landscapes of Singapore
Published by: Mr & Mrs Z Pte Ltd Publishing

Printed in Singapore
ISBN: 978-981-18-7808-4 (Hardcover)

Design and Project Management
Redbean De Pte Ltd

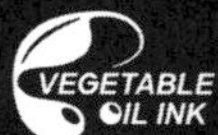

This book is printed on paper from sustainable forest, using 100% clean energy and vegetable oil ink.